CONTENTS

Veterinary college enrollment. Working with veterinarians. Expanding opportunities. A broader picture. Contributions to human health.

Ancient civilizations. Premodern history. The eighteenth and nineteenth centuries. The twentieth century.

Observing veterinarians at work. Personal assessment. High school preparation. College. Designing a preveterinary curriculum. Veterinary medical education. Professional standards. Gaining admission to a veterinary college. Criteria used for the selection of applicants. Veterinary Medical College Application Service. Financing a veterinary education. Scholarships and loans. Continuing education and graduate studies.

General practitioners. Contract practice. Partnership practice. Group practice. Specialty practices. The veterinary hospital. Small-animal practice. Zoo veterinarians. Expected income. A license to practice. Foreign veterinary graduates.

United States Department of Agriculture. U.S. Public Health Service. Affiliated federal agencies. Communicable disease research. Educational requirements. United States Food and Drug Administration. Public service at the state and local levels. Veterinarians as specialists. Veterinarians in world service. Providing assistance abroad. Agency for International Development. Role of the USDA. International cooperation. Involvement in the Americas. The Peace Corps.

Veterinarians in the drug industry. Veterinarians in the food industry. Other industry opportunities.

Rewards of academic work. Research agencies and categories. Link between human and animal health. The extension veterinarian. Laboratory animal medicine. Scientific organizations. AVMA positions on animals used in research and teaching.

History of the Veterinary Corps. VETCOM. Disease prevention. Dogs and horses. 91T training.

VGM Opportunities Series

OPPORTUNITIES IN
VETERINARY
MEDICINE CAREERS

Robert E. Swope

Revised by
Julie Rigby

Foreword by
Leonard F. Seda, D.V.M.
President
American Veterinary Medical Association

 **VGM Career Books**

12813986

Library of Congress Cataloging-in-Publication Data

Swope, Robert E.
    Opportunities in veterinary medicine careers / Robert E. Swope.—Rev. ed. /
by Julie Rigby.
        p. cm. — (VGM opportunities series)
    ISBN 0-658-01054-9 (hardcover)
    ISBN 0-658-01055-7 (paperback)
        1. Veterinary medicine—Vocational guidance. 2. Veterinary medicine—
Vocational guidance—United States. I. Rigby, Julie. II. Title. III. Series.

SF756.28 .S96 2001
636.089'023—dc21

                                                                    00-53373

Published by VGM Career Books
A division of The McGraw-Hill Companies.
4255 West Touhy Avenue, Lincolnwood (Chicago), Illinois 60712-1975 U.S.A.
Copyright © 2001 by The McGraw-Hill Companies.
Printed in the United States of America
International Standard Book Number: 0-658-01054-9 (hardcover)
                                     0-658-01055-7 (paperback)

1   2   3   4   5   6   7   8   9   0   LB/LB   0   9   8   7   6   5   4   3   2   1

ABOUT THE AUTHOR

Robert E. Swope actively participated in student affairs for more than two decades, serving as an academic advisor for undergraduate preveterinary students and counseling hundreds of students in the biological sciences. Formerly a Professor of Veterinary Science and Assistant Dean for Resident Education at Pennsylvania State University, he also conducted research on bovine diseases.

Fully acquainted with the breadth and depth of contemporary veterinary science, Dr. Swope served as a veterinary advisor on assignment in India and Chile on three occasions. A member of the American Veterinary Medical Association and the United States Animal Health Association, the author also conducted research and diagnostic work at the University of Maryland and served with the U.S. Army Veterinary Corps. Dr. Swope received his V.M.D. (Doctor of Veterinary Medicine) from the University of Pennsylvania.

Julie Rigby is a freelance writer living in Vermont.

FOREWORD

A career in veterinary medicine offers opportunities in a wide variety of professional areas, including public health, care of companion and food animals, government service, research, and many others. A large percentage of veterinarians also work in private clinical practice. No matter what area of expertise, however, the link that bonds all veterinarians is their ability and aptitude for problem solving and the fact that they all thoroughly enjoy doing it.

Veterinarians want to know why. As scientists they possess an inquisitive nature, and as clinicians they want to find practical applications for their knowledge.

The unique challenges of a medical/scientific career are now being augmented with computer technology, which helps veterinarians develop and manage more information. These advancements present enormous opportunities for applications in the diagnosis and treatment of animals as well as human members in the family. The ability to communicate with both the patient and the owner or guardian is extremely important in the veterinary profession.

Veterinarians must possess a love of animals, and they need to enjoy and have respect for human relationships. Veterinary medicine is a diverse profession that provides its members with not only the means to earn a living, but a lifetime of fulfillment and personal growth. It is my sincere wish that your career choice provides you with the opportunity for developing lifelong friendships and a sense of both personal and professional satisfaction and success.

Leonard F. Seda, D.V.M.
President
American Veterinary Medical Association

CHAPTER 1

THE WORLD OF VETERINARY MEDICINE

> If you decide to become a veterinary surgeon you will never grow rich, but you will have a life of endless interest and variety.

> —James Herriot

Do you enjoy being with animals? Are you the kind of person who volunteers to walk the dog, groom the horse, or even handle the classroom snake or rat? Or maybe you are intrigued by news reports of the work of veterinarians in the field of infectious diseases that affect wild animals, livestock, and even humans. Perhaps you have had an opportunity to observe a veterinarian at work and have decided to pursue a career dedicated to promoting the health of a wide range of domesticated animals.

If you feel comfortable working with animals, that's a good start for a future in veterinary medicine. But it is only a start. Veterinary medicine belongs to the field of medical science, and as such it requires years of education before one can assume the mantle of a Doctor of Veterinary Medicine.

Veterinarians put in long hours, often dealing with very difficult and complex issues. A veterinarian may spend his or her work hours tromping around in frozen mud taking care of dairy cows or may be called upon to euthanize a badly injured or critically ill pet dog or cat.

If even the worst-case scenarios don't scare you off, congratulations. The world of veterinary medicine is above all an extremely rewarding field, one that provides high job satisfaction and interesting challenges. Those who enter veterinary school belong to a select group of high-achieving students, individuals who have been encouraged by their teachers and guidance counselors to pursue one of the most varied scientific careers. Your fellow veterinary candidates all have a strong background in the biological sciences and a consuming desire to learn more about the various issues affecting the health of animals.

Opportunities abound for dedicated students of veterinary medicine. Veterinarians are employed by a wide range of organizations, and they care for an equally vast number of species—from the hippopotamus in the local zoo to the canine forces of the U.S. military, to the elite racehorses worth millions of dollars—not to mention countless dogs, cats, rabbits, birds, and other household pets. Veterinarians are also exploring the frontiers of research. For example, in 1999 veterinarians led the investigation into the causes of an outbreak of West Nile virus in New York state, tracing the cases of deadly human encephalitis to a rare virus infecting birds. Other ongoing research includes work on cancer, epilepsy, leukemia, and other diseases in animals and people; explorations in genetic engineering and cloning; and new techniques for surgical intervention for injured animals. Veterinarians are also intimately involved in working to increase the productivity of domesticated animals to meet the world's rising demand for food, as well as helping to preserve species that are endangered by the human population explosion and the destruction of the animals' natural habitats.

Is veterinary medicine for you? The hours are long, and no doubt there is more money to be made in other lines of work. And maybe it is not always as romantic as the wonderful memoirs of James Herriot, author of *All Creatures Great and Small* and other books about his life as a veterinarian in rural England. Yet ask a practicing veterinarian what he or she likes most about the profession, and you are likely to hear that the appeal of veterinary medicine lies in its variety, the opportunities for lifelong learning, and the satisfaction that can come only from applying one's self to a challenging task.

VETERINARY COLLEGE ENROLLMENT

The great strides made in veterinary medicine at the close of the twentieth century created more opportunities for future veterinarians to receive a cutting-edge, challenging education. In the last twenty years the number of excellent veterinary medical colleges in the United States and Canada has grown to twenty-seven.

Another important development was the entrance of women into the ranks of veterinarians. Where only a few decades ago it was virtually unheard of for women to become veterinarians, by the end of the twentieth century more women than men were studying veterinary medicine in the United States. The trend's growth was extremely rapid. In 1970 women made up only 10 percent of all students enrolled in veterinary colleges. By 1999, however, 70 percent of all veterinary students were women. That year, there were 9,055 veterinary students in the United States alone; of these, 2,759 were men and 6,296 were women.

The increasing number of female veterinary students is ultimately changing the face of veterinary practice. In 1991 there were 37,200 men and 11,500 women working as veterinarians in the United States. By 1999, as some of the older veterinarians retired and more recent graduates entered the field, women made up 34 percent of the 45,200 veterinarians in private practice and 43 percent of the 10,180 employed by government organizations and corporations!

While the situation for women who wish to become veterinarians has improved dramatically, there are still gains to be made in opportunities for minority students. According to the American Association of Veterinary Medical Colleges, there were a total of 6,695 applicants to veterinary schools in 1999. Of these, 5,648 were identified as Caucasian. Only 135 applicants were identified as African-American, 226 as Hispanic, 55 as Native American, 204 as Asian, and another 88 as "other." In order to promote greater diversity in the field, veterinary educators are working to encourage more minority students to consider this exciting and rewarding profession.

WORKING WITH VETERINARIANS

Suppose you are interested in working with animals, but do not wish to pursue the rigorous and time-consuming course of study required to become a veterinarian. The related field of veterinary technology is a great option open to those who want to work with animals under the supervision of a veterinarian. This career path does not require the clinical medical knowledge that veterinarians must have, and training as a veterinary technician can usually be completed in a two-year program after high school. Veterinary technicians are an integral part of any veterinary practice, performing medical tests on animals, preparing and delivering vaccines and other injections, and assisting with surgical procedures. Opportunities in this rapidly growing profession are found throughout the country, as well as in the military. (See Appendix B for a list of veterinary technology programs.)

EXPANDING OPPORTUNITIES

Veterinarians have always been involved in much more than the routine care of domestic animals. Yet by the beginning of the twenty-first century, the role of veterinarians has grown to encompass even more challenges and opportunities.

Veterinarians play an increasingly critical role in agricultural production, ensuring that the food on our tables comes from healthy animals. They monitor the humane transportation and slaughter of animals and check to see that animals used for food both here and abroad are disease-free.

Approximately 50 percent of our foodstuffs are derived from animals in the form of meat and dairy products—everything ranging from cattle and pork to fish, eggs, milk, and cheese. In the last ten years, in fact, the range of animal products available in the United States has expanded to include free-range bison and eggs from emus. By the beginning of the twenty-first century, the number of people on earth passed the six billion mark. Faced with this population explosion, agriculture at home and abroad must produce more livestock to meet the growing need for food and other animal products, including the materials from animals that we use to manufacture clothing. Livestock producers rely on veterinarians to increase their productivity; the success or failure of a livestock operation may often hinge on the effectiveness of a veterinarian. Similarly, consumers count on veterinarians to ensure that the animals used in livestock operations are treated humanely and with an eye toward creating healthy food products.

A BROADER PICTURE

American veterinarians have made historic contributions to the advancement of both agriculture and public health.

They also have a tradition of sharing new knowledge, practices, and technology with people beyond our national borders, providing assistance and advice to underdeveloped nations. These nations are striving to implement the same standards for livestock production and human health that exist in the United States. Veterinary medicine is, therefore, playing a key role in such development.

Students exploring careers in veterinary medicine are often unaware of the tremendous challenges and opportunities in this field. People generally acquire an image of veterinarians through contact with their local veterinarian. For the urban youth, this contact is generally limited to small-animal practitioners, who constitute about half of the veterinarians in this country. While the percentage of small-animal practitioners (the dog and cat doctors) is growing, there are other veterinarians who lead exciting professional lives, sometimes working overseas with quite different animal populations, or in the United States with large or exotic animals.

Currently, there are almost 70,000 veterinarians in the United States and Canada. A total of twenty-seven veterinary schools and colleges enrolled more than 8,500 potential veterinarians in 1999. That same year, more than 2,000 students received their doctoral degrees in veterinary medicine.

In economic terms, veterinary professionals oversee in excess of 200 million head of livestock that have an economic value of well over $50 billion. Veterinarians are also responsible for the health of more than 52 million dogs, at a cost of about $128.77 per dog per year. In addition to the number of dogs, more than 59 million cats were examined by veterinarians during 1999. The feline population is growing quite quickly, and it is estimated that on average the medical expenses per cat are about $81 per year. Bird ownership has also grown in recent years, to more than 13 million birds in 1999. And veterinarians also treat the 4 million horses, 5.7 million rabbits and ferrets, 4.8 million rodents, and 3.5 million reptiles we keep as pets!

CONTRIBUTIONS TO HUMAN HEALTH

Veterinary medicine plays a significant role in the human health-care delivery system. Veterinarians' activities are often directly related to human beings. Veterinarians help identify and prevent the outbreak and spread of animal diseases, some of which, like rabies, can be transmitted to human beings. In addition, veterinarians are involved in food protection, as well as the prevention and control of environmental hazards. They also work on scientific research teams on such projects as searching out new pharmaceuticals to treat human heart disease. The military services have commissioned almost 450 veterinary officers to meet the food inspection and other public health requirements of military personnel and their families at home and abroad. In addition, the military veterinarian may engage in new research frontiers (see Chapter 8).

The impact of environmental health hazards and food-borne diseases upon human health has received increasing attention. The control of the ingestion of toxic chemicals by livestock has become a high priority objective as laboratory research reveals their harmful effects on human health. More than ever, there is a need for veterinarians who will be able to deal with chemical contamination of the food chain. As well, veterinarians are asked to provide expertise on other public health concerns, such as the use of growth hormones or bioengineering in livestock.

CHAPTER 2

HISTORY OF VETERINARY MEDICINE

The practice of veterinary medicine is one of the oldest scientific skills developed by humans. During the Paleolithic period prior to 8000 B.C., our ancestors lived in a symbiotic relationship with the wild animals around them, hunting them for food, clothing, and other materials necessary for survival. Animals had not yet been domesticated, except possibly the dog. Survival depended on hunting a variety of animals, which included sheep, cows, horses, and pigs. One can easily imagine an ancient hunter caring for a dog that helps him on his hunt, although no archaeological evidence from this period has yet been discovered that suggests this sort of prehistoric veterinary care.

The domestication of animals and the development of agriculture began between 3000–2500 B.C. The first farm animals to be domesticated were pigs, followed by sheep, goats, horses, and oxen, which could be used for working in the fields as well as for food. Although animals had always had diseases in the wild, people had not lived in close enough contact with them to recognize these diseases or formulate remedies against them. But once the animals were domesticated, ensuring their health became a real priority. Not only were the animals important because they provided the means of survival, they were also highly esteemed by primitive people. For this reason, caring for them became a matter of great concern to the early agriculturalists, although there are no records telling the stories of the successes and failures of the first veterinarians.

ANCIENT CIVILIZATIONS

Records from the early Egyptian, Babylonian, and Hindu civilizations do provide some insights into ancient veterinary knowledge. The evidence indicates that veterinary medicine was given the same place in the society as human medicine. Much of the veterinary record is interspersed with information on human disease, an early sign of recognition of the close correlation of human and animal medicine.

Egypt

Fascinating material has been preserved through the ages that shows the early specialization of veterinary medicine. In ancient Egypt, poultry, cat, and dog specialists offered specialized services, and those charged with the care of cattle were especially burdened with responsibility, since the loss of one of these sacred animals was more serious than that of a human life. Horses were also highly valued as military animals, and specialists in the ills of horses were commissioned for service in the Egyptian armies.

Because of its role as a center of commerce, Egypt was the crossroads for the spread of animal disease. The Bible at the time of Israelite captivity in Egypt describes plagues of lice, flies, murrain (anthrax), boils, hail, and locusts that ravaged both people and animals or destroyed their food supplies. Moses was perhaps one of the first to establish regulations for the isolation or quarantine of diseased animals—the basic concept of preventive medicine.

The Code of Hammurabi provided for the legal regulation of the practices of veterinary and human medicine. It determined the punishment for a veterinarian's carelessness or neglect; thus a veterinary surgeon who caused the death of an ox or ass would be required to pay a quarter of the animal's value to its owner. In addition to a code of ethics, it required the recording of diseases as they appeared to the practitioner and established fixed fees for most services performed.

India

One must turn to India to find the most effectual and lasting beginnings to the veterinary art. In the old Brahman Vedas, dated about 1800 B.C., veterinary specialization is described. Ayurveda, the science of life, included veterinary medicine as well as human medicine. In ancient agrarian India, a society in which it was believed that people and animals traveled the same road to destiny, animals were given a place of high esteem. During this period, cattle were the most prized possession, and the concept of reincarnation and the sacred position of the cow arose from this close kinship between humans and animals. Veterinary hospitals were established about 250 B.C., and government edicts governed the practices of the Indian veterinarian. These government-sponsored hospitals are much in evidence in India today, and only in India are "gosadans" or "old cow homes" provided for the care of the older animal.

The life of people in India in the second century B.C. was closely bound together with animal life. The slaughter of animals was prohibited, cruelty to animals was subject to severe punishment, and animal owners were required to give detailed accounts of diseases or deaths of animals. Selective breeding, genetics, and the study of aging (geriatrics) were carefully applied to animal as well as to human medicine. Surgery and obstetrics were given foremost attention, and some of the methods described are among those still in use today. India maintained its place as the leading authority in veterinary medicine until the tenth century A.D., when the art and science of animal health fell into complete oblivion until it was revived by the British some eight hundred years later.

Greece

The history of veterinary medicine now turns to Greece. While ancient Greek medicine is well documented, beginning with Aesculapius (1250 B.C.), little is known of Greek veterinary medicine until the writings of Hippocrates in the fourth century B.C. Under the guidance of Hippocrates, modern medicine was born, with the ethics, means of reporting, and rational treatments that are familiar to us today. Hippocrates became a student of comparative anatomy and pathology, recognizing some of the similarities between people and animals.

Ancient Rome

Despite medical beginnings shrouded in mysticism, which attributed events in human affairs to the actions of gods, the Roman empire saw a growth in knowledge about the healing arts. This era marks an important page in veterinary history. "Professional" medicine reached Rome from Greece in the third century B.C., but veterinary medicine did not receive full attention until the first century A.D. Before then, Roman civilization, possessing little regard for medicine itself, had, for economic reasons, less interest in animals and their care.

As Roman appreciation of agriculture improved, however, their attitude toward livestock was reversed. Animal husbandry became a primary occupation among the agricultural community, and techniques for animal isolation and quarantine, sanitation, and concepts of disease transmission (particularly concerning the dreaded disease, rabies), were well established. Purely Roman contributions to the field of veterinary medicine failed to develop, and since they lacked the creativity to progress beyond their Greek inheritances, veterinary medicine soon fell, like the Empire itself, into a state of decline. Only Galen, a Greek physician practicing in Rome, can be counted as a member of this civilization who contributed measurably to veterinary progress. Galen was the original anatomist and physiologist, and his recorded observations were based on dissections of Roman military horses.

Byzantium

The Byzantine Empire, centered in Constantinople, but nevertheless Greek in all respects, produced the voluminous collections of veterinary writings, the *Hippiatrika,* representing a compilation of observations on the veterinary art by actual practitioners of that era. One of the principal contributors to the *Hippiatrika* was Apsyrtus, who along with Vegetius, shares the title of "father of veterinary medicine." Apsyrtus was the leading veterinarian of his day and personally described many of the medical and surgical problems associated with the horse. Although Vegetius was not a veterinarian, he provided an accurate presentation of the veterinary art in his time. While basic conceptions still reverted to those originating with the Greeks, Vegetius did add some of his own original descriptions, expanding on Apsyrtus's commentaries by applying knowledge gained through experiences with horses and cattle. When Vegetius's pleas for the cause of veterinary medicine went unheeded, the art of animal care virtually fell into oblivion for the next thousand years.

PREMODERN HISTORY

Dark Ages

The Dark Ages were characterized by destructive plagues that appeared in France, Ireland, Britain, Germany, and other parts of Europe. Unfortunately, the response to these plagues did not produce any new concepts or practices concerning the causes, nature, or the means of treatment and eradication of disease.

However, from the twelfth to the fifteenth century, a tremendous revival of learning took place in Europe, with renewed interest in medicine on the part of nobility and the scholars of the day. Medical education gained support, and though the veterinary art remained in the hands of untrained horseshoers, the first glimmer of inquisitiveness concerning veterinary science began to appear in the contemporary literature. From a practical viewpoint, however, devastating animal plagues continued unchecked throughout most of Europe, primarily because of a lack of adequately trained and properly motivated veterinarians.

Renaissance

Toward the end of the Renaissance, a period known for discovery and invention, progress in the physical and natural sciences served as a stimulus to veterinary medicine. With Spain in the center of the stage, the profession experienced a reawakening. Spain's leadership in the field was soon to disappear, but other countries, particularly England and France, gathered the necessary enthusiasm to establish themselves as the true founders of modern veterinary science.

THE EIGHTEENTH AND NINETEENTH CENTURIES

The First Veterinary School

Despite the erratic beginnings of veterinary medicine, the field began to be recognized as a distinct branch of higher learning during the eighteenth century. With the establishment in 1762 of the first government-sponsored veterinary school in Lyon, France, the door was opened for veterinary practitioners throughout Europe to apply the science of veterinary medicine to their long-existing art.

The well-established agricultural economy was regularly beset with setbacks that required the expertise of trained veterinarians. Rinderpest outbreaks among European cattle resulted in the death of 200 million cattle in the first half of the eighteenth century. Pleuropneumonia in cattle, glanders and influenza in horses, pox in sheep, and rabies and distemper in dogs were rampant during this period. Obviously many of the animal diseases, particularly anthrax and rabies, were also taking their toll on the human population.

Out of this chaos, the profession of veterinary medicine emerged. Concepts were developed concerning disease transmission and the means by which disease outbreaks might be prevented or controlled. Isolation of animals in infested localities, proper sanitary care of carcasses, and separation of healthy animals from sick ones were all accepted as common practice and undoubtedly contributed greatly to the final eradication of certain diseases.

The Nineteenth Century

In the early 1800s, European veterinarians and farriers immigrated to the United States and Canada. At this time, the economy of United States revolved almost exclusively around agriculture. Though livestock production was not as central as it is to our agricultural economy today, interest in veterinary service was high.

By the onset of the Civil War, agriculturalists throughout the country were organized, specialized, and in most cases, self-sufficient. American inventiveness led to better machinery, transportation, and marketing procedures. Farming, for the most part, was a profitable business, and landowners were looking for contributions from science to provide the means for further improvements in agriculture.

U.S. Government Agencies

The federal government recognized its role in advancing national agricultural production with the creation of the United States Department of Agriculture (USDA) in 1862. With the establishment of the USDA, a formal, well-financed approach to the problems of the livestock industry could be undertaken. At the time, cattle plague, foot-and-mouth disease, rinderpest, and other ravaging diseases continued in Europe. American livestock were not immune to disease. Destructive plagues, including hog cholera, pleuropneumonia, anthrax, and sheep pox, were reported throughout the country. During the Civil War, the movement of soldiers and animals aggravated the existing disease problems and created new ones. After several unsuccessful attempts at organization, the U.S. Veterinary Medical Association, now the American Veterinary Medical Association (AVMA), was founded in 1863. Its objective was "to contribute to the diffusion of true science and particularly the knowledge of veterinary medicine and surgery."

Land Grant College Act

In 1862 the passage of the Morrill Land Grant College Act provided for "federal appropriation to the states of a portion of public lands for the advancement of agriculture and the mechanical arts." This act made formal education available for students in veterinary science. With financial support, organization, and educational facilities, the field of veterinary medicine was finally given the money and the impetus to move ahead.

In the first decade following the Civil War, much effort was spent in determining the exact position and responsibility of these three newly created parents of modern veterinary medicine, namely the USDA, the AVMA, and the land-grant colleges. Studies by the Department of Agriculture revealed that pleuropneumonia was being spread westward by the movement of cattle from the South, and blackleg, abortion, glanders, tetanus, hog cholera, foot rot, parasitic disease, and other diseases were taking their toll of livestock far beyond any previously existing estimates.

The early annual Department of Agriculture reports of animal diseases accelerated plans by several of the land-grant colleges to transform their veterinary science departments into colleges of veterinary medicine. The first public-supported veterinary college opened at Iowa State College in 1879. Among the privately owned schools formed during the late nineteenth century, only the school at the University of Pennsylvania is still in existence.

AVMA Contributions

The AVMA also contributed to the advancement of veterinary science by providing a means of communication and exchange of ideas among veterinarians through annual scientific meetings and the publication of the *American Veterinary Review.* The leaders were, for the most part, farsighted individuals who recognized that the science of veterinary medicine allowed the practitioner much more scope in caring for the sick animal. They also understood the necessity of the herd or mass approach to disease prevention and control to avert disease and preserve livestock health.

Bureau of Animal Industry

In 1884 another milestone was passed with the enactment of the Hatch Act, creating the Bureau of Animal Industry within the Department of Agriculture. The bureau was specifically charged with the prevention of importation of diseased cattle and the suppression of contagious pleuropneumonia, by far the most persistent of the cattle diseases, and other contagious diseases among domestic animals. Congressman Hatch also sponsored bills that provided for federal support to state agricultural colleges for scientific research in all fields of agriculture, including veterinary medicine, and for the establishment of the Meat Inspection Act of 1890.

Following strenuous and successful efforts aimed at eradicating contagious pleuropneumonia, the Bureau of Animal Industry turned its attention to what was to become perhaps the most exciting and significant veterinary research during these late years of the nineteenth century. As early as 1750, in the southeastern colonies, serious cattle losses had been encountered from the effects of a peculiar plague. The means by which the disease spread was not known, but recognition of contagion prompted quarantine measures that served to partially inhibit movement of this cattle disease. The disease appeared again in Texas in 1854 and was named "Texas fever."

Mystery of the Tick

As the cattle from Texas were driven to northern markets, new avenues of transmission of the contagious disease were formed. Northern livestock officials refused to accept the infected cattle and most outlets for southern cattle were closed. Illegal means of moving cattle were found, however, and the disease continued to threaten the entire livestock industry shortly after the Civil War. Livestock handlers were the first to offer a clue as to the actual means of transmission, for as losses were reported, mention was made of the presence of lice and ticks on the bodies of diseased animals. The relationship remained obscure until Dr. D. E. Salmon, Chief of the Bureau of Animal Industry, established a geographical distribution of the disease that firmly proved that the disease area corresponded very closely with the habitat of the tick.

F. L. Kilborne and Theobold Smith, under Salmon's supervision, finally unraveled the mystery of the tick. Kilborne, the veterinarian, conceived and conducted the first experiments that proved that the tick was, in fact, the biological vector in transmission of Texas fever. Smith, the physician-pathologist, demonstrated that the actual causative agent was a blood parasite. Cooper Curtice, Kilborne's veterinary colleague, worked out the life cycle of the tick and urged the development of a program whereby the century-old tick-borne disease could be eradicated from the United States. The work of Salmon, Kilborne, Smith, Curtice, and many others had a tremendous impact on future studies in animal and human disease.

Malaria and the Panama Canal

Malaria, a terrible and often fatal disease that had affected human populations throughout the world for several centuries, remained unchecked until researchers established the role of insects in the transmission of disease. This discovery helped make the construction of the Panama Canal possible. Before this, the fatality rate for workers on the canal was extremely high. Veterinarians and others discovered that yellow fever, typhus, bubonic plague, and many other insect-borne diseases could be brought under control.

The problems created by Texas fever were also partly responsible for the founding of an organization composed of livestock owners and veterinarians, known today as the United States Animal Health Association. Needless to say, since the last part of the nineteenth century the profession has made great leaps forward, and its success, respect, and prestige have multiplied many times over.

THE TWENTIETH CENTURY

As veterinary medicine entered the twentieth century, it found a place in the rapidly growing and prosperous livestock industry. Many of the major diseases were now under control or eradicated, and livestock owners found that with improved veterinary service the raising of livestock could provide a profitable livelihood. Veterinary practitioners, graduates of the new schools founded during the late nineteenth century, were now recognized as an integral and essential part of the society. The rise in stature of veterinarians during the twentieth century was prompted by many new and different challenges and by leadership with unusual ingenuity and foresight.

Among the disease problems during this period were hemorrhagic septicemia in swine, swamp fever in horses, and the ever-present hog cholera. The attack on brucellosis, a serious, debilitating disease transmitted from animals to humans, had to be postponed until 1939, when diagnostic techniques, vaccination procedures, and breeding management paved the way for an eradication program. By enlisting the cooperative efforts of a large portion of the veterinarians in this country, the disease has been virtually eliminated in humans and markedly reduced in its incidence among animals.

Tuberculosis Eradication

The type of veterinary effort represented in the campaign against brucellosis had its first real test in the tuberculosis eradication program instituted by Dr. John R. Mohler in 1917. A diagnostic test was developed that could detect this disease in its early stages, which prompted the destruction of infected animals. Although this seemingly drastic measure met with considerable opposition at the time, few could question its value when its full effects were realized upon complete eradication of the disease in 1940.

Mohler summed up its benefits in the following quote:

> The medical profession is keenly interested in the aggressive methods used to combat animal diseases. The banker, once skeptical about financing purebred cattle, now lends support to such activities. The housewife recognizes that meat, properly inspected, is now one of the most wholesome foods for her family. Such goodwill naturally has far-reaching economic importance, but more important is the stimulating effect on those of us who have selected some branch of the industry as our life's work. The pride of service adds richly to our lives in helping to better livestock conditions, in increasing our national wealth, in protecting public health, and in adding to the comfort and happiness of rural life. The conquest of tuberculosis was a true milestone in veterinary history.

The era of the mid-thirties produced other significant advances in veterinary medicine. By 1933, interest in small-animal medicine and the accompanying increase in veterinary hospitals led to the founding of the American Animal Hospital Association, the first organization devoted to improving professional service and facilities for the care of small animals.

During this period, the objectives and philosophy of veterinary service underwent careful scrutiny and analysis. Previously, nearly all veterinary activities had been closely related to agriculture, and any contact with other disciplines was the exception rather than the rule. This was soon to change.

Without separating itself from the agricultural sciences, by the middle of the twentieth century veterinary medicine gradually began to consider itself as one of the medical sciences. While this concept was challenged by many members of the profession, most came to realize that veterinarians, by virtue of their training and skills, were faced with new responsibilities concerning not only the treatment and prevention of animal diseases but human health as well.

The Development of Modern Veterinary Science

At the beginning of the twenty-first century, those responsible for the maintenance of animal and human health are continually cultivating a better understanding of their common problems. Human medicine looks to studies in animals for guidance in handling disease problems in the human population. Veterinary research will continue to provide many of the answers necessary for the alleviation of human ills. This emphasis on linking veterinary medicine to human health gained momentum just prior to World War II, when research focusing on the interrelationships between human and veterinary health problems began to appear in the professional literature. The profession was taking a new look at its possible course for the future.

Every effort was made to develop policy and promote public relations directed toward improvement and expansion of services. Many veterinarians called to military duty during the war needed to apply the broad knowledge received during their veterinary education and use this knowledge under a variety of adverse conditions. The contributions of members of the Army Veterinary Corps provided additional evidence that the modern veterinarian was a "new breed," well-trained in many facets of the health sciences.

Post–World War II

Following the war, a new challenge faced American veterinarians: the possibility of the introduction of foot-and-mouth disease into the United States from Mexico. Responding promptly, the Bureau of Animal Industry personnel assisted Mexican authorities in controlling the disease. Brucellosis continued to be a problem until 1961, when an eradication campaign extending over twenty years finally culminated in the eradication of the disease. Control campaigns continue with this disease, as well as with tuberculosis, in order to avoid any future threat to livestock.

During the second half of the twentieth century the veterinary profession gradually assumed a pivotal role in the advance of research in the medical uses of atomic energy; in the control of zoonoses, or diseases common to humans and animals; in studies on the immunological relationships of viruses in humans and animals; in the public health significance of residual antibiotics in food products; in efforts to overcome the toxicity of pesticides needed to maintain a high yield of food production; in the development of tranquilizers, corticosteroids, and other drugs that have common animal and human use; in the space-medicine research program; in studies on exotic diseases existing in foreign countries that could threaten our own livestock economy; and in numerous other challenges.

CHAPTER 3

PREPARING FOR YOUR FUTURE AS A VETERINARIAN

How can a person determine if veterinary medicine is the right career to pursue? Often, people know from an early age that they would like to work in the field of animal health. For many veterinarians, their earliest and fondest memories are of taking care of neighborhood animals, from abandoned baby birds to local household pets. Those who grow up on working farms recall the hours spent tending to cows, sheep, horses, and pigs. Most veterinarians can't quite pinpoint the exact moment when they decided to study veterinary medicine. Instead, the dream of working with animals has always been a part of their lives.

The difference between those who dream of becoming a veterinarian, and those who do, is a matter of intensity, concentration, and discipline. By high school a candidate for veterinary medicine must show a strong aptitude in science and research, as well as a dedicated work ethic. In short, the future veterinarian is one who demonstrates a continuous level of interest in the subject, as he or she is then more likely to sustain this enthusiasm through the long years of medical training and scholarship.

OBSERVING VETERINARIANS AT WORK

One of the most effective ways to acquire a well-informed view of the profession is to be exposed to the rigors and routines of the veterinary practice. Most veterinarians are willing to advise young people who are seriously interested in a career in veterinary medicine. Indeed, there are a wealth of opportunities to gain work experience in a veterinary practice. Many veterinarians hire high school students to work after school; these students contribute to the day-to-day functioning of the clinic, whether it is a city-based small animal practice, or a large animal or mixed practice in the suburbs or countryside.

There is only one way to gain this valuable work experience: Ask for it. Those who are acquainted with a veterinarian who has taken care of their family pets already have an introduction. Even if a student does not personally know a veterinarian, it is still always advisable to apply for a job. Many students are hired to help take care of animals that are staying in veterinary kennels; this work consists of cleaning cages, walking dogs, and helping maintain the veterinary clinic. At many practices, student employees are also involved in assisting in the examining room. Although the work is sometimes dirty or not that exciting, it is very beneficial to have this kind of exposure, as it helps measure the depth of one's interest in the field. Indeed, even if there is no renumeration for the work, the privilege of working for a veterinarian should be accepted, as this sort of experience is priceless. Moreover, many veterinary colleges require an apprenticeship with a veterinarian as a prerequisite to admission.

If it is not possible to locate employment in a veterinary practice, students should seek out other opportunities to work with animals, such as volunteering at a local animal shelter or working on a farm during summer vacations.

PERSONAL ASSESSMENT

Veterinary medicine is a demanding field, so it is necessary to assess one's own character and aptitudes to determine whether an individual is suited for the profession.

A strong constitution is necessary, as is physical stamina and strength, as veterinary practice necessitates long, arduous working hours, often under adverse conditions. However, brute strength is not required. One of the leading equine veterinarians is a petite woman who had to work hard to convince farmers and horse investors she was truly capable of working with their animals. Obviously, young veterinarians who have been reared on a farm have some initial advantage over the urbanite in a large-animal practice. This fact, however, should not discourage the city dweller, who can gain the necessary confidence for handling livestock through experience.

The veterinarian must have an inquiring and studious mind, and must be ready for constant reeducation on new developments and techniques that provide for greater simplicity and effectiveness. This includes the reading of current veterinary periodicals and participating in professional meetings.

Among other attributes expected of any professional person are an ability to communicate in oral and written form, sincerity, honesty, tact, respect for one's colleagues, and good business sense. All of these qualities are necessary in building a successful practice, in working as a member of a research team or as a teacher, or in any other aspect of the veterinary profession.

HIGH SCHOOL PREPARATION

A broad college-preparatory program in high school allows students to keep their options open. Their high school program should include as much college-track work as possible, especially in mathematics, computer programming, and the sciences, such as chemistry, biology, and physics, which provide a strong familiarity with scientific methodologies. Communications skills are also of special importance. Taking four years of high school English is highly recommended. Foreign language proficiency is often not required but would add to a broad educational background. In addition to the basic academic courses, additional work in bookkeeping and business law would be helpful if a person's schedule permits their addition.

Students are also encouraged, as time allows, to engage in extracurricular activities: biological science and chemistry clubs, science fairs, 4-H activities, as well as special summer enrichment programs in science or math. Completing a high school program that will lead to university admission requires continuous academic work of a high calibre.

COLLEGE

The student should carefully consider the selection of a college or university for undergraduate preparation for admission to veterinary school. All veterinary colleges require a minimum of two years of preprofessional training for admission. However, students generally complete three, four, or more years of college education before gaining admission.

Generally speaking, this training again consists of biological and physical sciences, social sciences, and communication skills. Although these courses may be taken at most liberal arts colleges, there are definite advantages to enrolling in a professional program associated with the college of agriculture at a state university. First, most of the state universities have a program specifically arranged to meet the particular needs of the veterinary schools, which have different requirements for admission. The affiliated preveterinary programs are up to date on trends and developments in veterinary education that necessitate occasional alterations in the program to provide a more adequate preparation.

Second, colleges of agriculture are able to offer the student basic and applied courses in disciplines related to the biological and physical sciences but oriented toward agriculture, such as animal management, nutrition, breeding, and agronomy. These courses provide a broader base of knowledge for students who have not yet decided what field of veterinary medicine they may wish to pursue after veterinary college.

Third, students should take advantage of the opportunity to associate themselves with the staff of veterinarians in the veterinary science departments of the agricultural college and/or the adjacent veterinary college. This allows them to receive authoritative and experienced guidance as they make their preparations to gain admission to veterinary school. In addition, sufficient numbers of students are enrolled in the preprofessional programs in most state institutions to justify a preveterinary club, which is sponsored by the faculty and provides for student-faculty fellowship and professional discussion.

State Universities

There are many advantages to attending a state university for preprofessional training in veterinary medicine. However, completion of such a program does not guarantee admission to the veterinary school at that same institution, as other factors also enter into the selection of veterinary students.

The choice of a preprofessional college may also depend on available funds to meet the expenses of the six- or seven-year combined program leading to the veterinary degree.

Students may complete as much undergraduate work as possible at an institution close to home to eliminate the expenses of living away from home. Students should always investigate the possibility of scholarships or loans at their chosen institution rather than accepting admission to a local institution that does not meet their educational objectives. Funds are generally available at most institutions for students who qualify academically and can provide evidence of genuine financial need. Similarly, ambitious and aggressive students can usually find part-time employment to defray at least a portion of their expenses.

DESIGNING A PREVETERINARY CURRICULUM

In undergraduate college, the student should take training beyond the minimum requirements for entrance into veterinary school. The value of a well-rounded education cannot be overstated. Courses in sciences, humanities, social studies, business, psychology, sociology, economics, the arts, and literature, as well as business management, financial management, and computer programming also would be helpful. Following completion of undergraduate studies, little or no opportunity may be available to students to expand their scope of learning in these directions. Many students today are electing to complete an entire four-year undergraduate baccalaureate program and receive the bachelor's degree prior to entering veterinary college.

Undergraduate students are advised to arrange for consultation with a teacher or administrator acquainted with veterinary college requirements, regardless of the undergraduate program in which they enrolled. Should admission to veterinary college become impossible, an informed adviser or counselor can make recommendations for the completion of an undergraduate program suitable to the individual student's interests and abilities with little or no loss of time and credit.

VETERINARY MEDICAL EDUCATION

Although veterinary medicine arose out of the need to care for sick animals, for economic or social reasons, it now reaches into many fields. Veterinary education, therefore, must encompass all of the biological and physical sciences. And as the profession changes, so must education in the field.

Before 1863, few practicing veterinarians in the United States had any formal training. Well into the twentieth century, two or three years in a veterinary school were sufficient to acquire the knowledge and skills to serve the needs of the livestock industry. Within the last few decades, greater emphasis has been placed on a broad preveterinary program to lay the foundations for the four-year veterinary curriculum, which is highly scientific. There is a large amount of material to be covered in four short years, a knowledge base that will serve as a foundation for future scholarship. However, true competence and depth in a specialized field can be acquired only by experience or postgraduate training.

PROFESSIONAL STANDARDS

All veterinary colleges in the United States and Canada must meet standards essential for veterinary colleges that have been established by the Council on Education of the American Veterinary Medical Association. The veterinary colleges maintain continual liaison with each other through the American Association of Veterinary Medical Colleges. In this manner, entrance requirements, curriculum changes, teaching methods, research facilities, libraries, and other intraprofessional relations can be discussed and a high degree of standardization among colleges maintained. Because the primary objective of a veterinary college is to educate competent veterinarians, graduates from all accredited institutions are then prepared to assume a variety of responsibilities.

Since education in basic science, laboratory, and clinical courses demands individual instruction, a ratio of one faculty member to each three students is maintained in all veterinary colleges. Many faculty members hold Master of Science and Doctor of Philosophy degrees in addition to the professional veterinary degree. Active research programs enhance the total educational offerings of the college. These programs are supported by federal and private grants and conducted by faculty with the assistance of graduate and undergraduate students.

The curriculum is essentially the same at each veterinary college and all confer the degree of Doctor of Veterinary Medicine (D.V.M.). The course work is in many respects similar to that required in medical schools. In general, the professional curriculum consists of two phases. In the first phase, students study preclinical sciences, such as bacteriology, histology, biochemistry, anatomy, physiology, pathology, microbiology, and pharmacology. The second phase of study focuses on clinical veterinary medicine. Students gain hands-on experience in a clinical setting treating animals, performing surgeries, and interacting with owners of animals.

Familiarity with All Species

While the student of human medicine must be acquainted with only one species, the veterinary student must learn all of the characteristics of many species—horse, cow, pig, sheep, dog, cat, poultry, and others. The normal structure and functions of the various organs must be understood before students can proceed to the abnormal conditions and changes that cause and result in clinical disease.

Third- and fourth-year students begin to handle animals under supervision, assisting in diagnosis, treatment, surgery, and laboratory techniques. Veterinary colleges maintain both large- and small-animal clinics catering to local livestock and pet owners. Practicing veterinarians often refer cases to these clinics for observation and study. In addition, senior students spend time on an ambulatory clinic making farm calls under graduate veterinary supervision. The junior and senior years are not without some classroom work, however. Radiology, veterinary law and ethics, food hygiene, public health, epidemiology, and obstetrics and gynecology are among the courses required.

Most veterinary colleges also encourage students to gain practical experience by working with practicing veterinarians during the summer months. Several colleges have organized internship programs that students must complete before receiving their degree. These programs provide the means whereby valuable experience can be gained under field conditions prior to the time when the young graduate must assume full responsibility.

GAINING ADMISSION TO A VETERINARY COLLEGE

Students interested in admission to veterinary colleges are frequently limited to those institutions located in their own, or adjoining, states. This should not imply that it is impossible to gain admission to other colleges, but such admission may be difficult.

There were twenty-seven approved veterinary medical colleges in the United States in 2000. Schools of veterinary medicine are located primarily in the states of the South and Midwest. The schools of veterinary medicine are located in twenty-six states. A number of schools have compact agreements that provide for admission of students from other states.

Although there has been a recent increase in applicants, many schools are willing to consider highly qualified applicants from states other than those with which they have compact agreements. Thus, while the competition for entrance is tough, the student who excels will still be in a good position to gain admittance to the college of his or her choice.

Certain institutions have acquired reputations for competence in particular veterinary disciplines, brought about by the presence of specially trained personnel on the staff and/or the fact that the geographical location of the college and its relationship to a livestock population may lend itself to the study of particular veterinary problems.

For example, clinical material for studies on diseases of range cattle and sheep is not available to nearly the same extent at Cornell University or the University of Pennsylvania as it is at Texas A&M, Colorado State University, or other western colleges. On the other hand, the eastern colleges have the advantage insofar as dairy cattle are concerned, while Purdue University and the universities of Illinois and Iowa undoubtedly provide increased opportunity for those interested in practical experience with swine.

Students would do well to visit the veterinary colleges to which they are applying. This provides an opportunity to speak with faculty members and current students and ask questions about the strengths of a particular veterinary program.

CRITERIA USED FOR THE SELECTION
OF APPLICANTS

Aside from some geographical-preference restrictions, several personal criteria are used by the veterinary colleges in the selection of a first-year class. Selection is based on those who possess a high potential for completion of the four-year program and subsequent success in pursuing a career in veterinary medicine.

Often, the best means of predicting students' futures is to measure their past performance. The veterinary colleges are primarily concerned with the academic records of the students. In addition to supplying information on courses taken and grades received, an academic record invariably carries with it some inferences or indications of students' general habits, ambitions, aggressiveness, and other characteristics.

Grades Are Important

While overall academic performance is considered, grades in the sciences are among the most reliable criteria for predicting success in the technical courses in veterinary college. Admissions committees also evaluate the applicants' interests in animals and their experience with them.

Since some colleges have specific farm practice requirements, students should seek advice on prerequisites from each college before enrolling. Summer employment between academic years in veterinary college can be aimed toward veterinary medicine. For those who did not gain early farm experience, these summer jobs should be rewarding and confirm a student's interest in farm practice.

With regard to employment in general, admissions committees are interested in the type of work, veterinary or nonveterinary, in which the applicants have been engaged during vacations or the school year. Ambitious and alert prospective veterinarians should seek out employment to prepare them for their chosen work. Not only the type of employment but also the interest and enthusiasm expressed in carrying out one's duties are evaluated by the committee.

Other Important Qualities

A pleasant noncombative personality is essential to anyone who provides a form of service to the public. Veterinarians must instill confidence in clients before clients can accept their knowledge. Admissions committees will invite applicants for an interview prior to final selection for admission in order to appraise a candidate's personal characteristics, motivations, and interests.

Several veterinary colleges require applicants to take the Veterinary Aptitude Test (Psychological Corporation, New York) or a similar test. Test results are forwarded to the veterinary schools of the students' choice and serve as an additional criterion in the selection of prospective veterinary students. Some schools now require the Graduate Record Examination (GRE), a commonly used test in graduate and professional schools to evaluate the students' undergraduate performance.

Thus, academic performance in high school and in an undergraduate college program; possession of honorable personal characteristics, including interest and motivation that fit the individual for a professional environment; part-time or summer employment experience; good health and stamina; and an overall competency in the biological and physical sciences, as exhibited in an aptitude test, are the primary considerations for one seeking admission to veterinary colleges.

VETERINARY MEDICAL COLLEGE APPLICATION SERVICE

The Veterinary Medical College Application Service (VMCAS), sponsored by the American Association of Veterinary Medical Colleges, serves as the central organization for distributing, collecting, and processing applications to veterinary school. Nearly every veterinary school participates in the VMCAS program. This service allows applicants to complete one application, which is then distributed to the schools chosen by the student. Admissions decisions are not made by VMCAS; the organization is also not involved with setting application, admission, or deadline requirements. Although the VMCAS booklet does instruct students on how to complete the VMCAS application, it is still important for students to independently research the veterinary medical colleges of their choice and determine if there are any additional application requirements not included in the VMCAS application.

For more information about VMCAS, write to:

Veterinary Medical College Application Service
1101 Vermont Avenue NW, Suite 411
Washington, DC 20005

FINANCING A VETERINARY EDUCATION

All things considered, the student who attends a public institution and resides at home can meet expenses most reasonably, while the student who selects a private institution away from home will generally be required to make the largest financial outlay.

Part-Time Employment

A student can defray at least some portion of these expenses, so that he or she does not graduate with a high burden of debt. Ambitious students often are able to assume part-time employment, but certain limitations must be placed on this activity. The work in professional school is quite demanding, and only the particularly good student can afford more than a few hours a week away from academic responsibilities. This is especially true during the freshman undergraduate year and again in the first year in veterinary school. These are two years that usually require a considerable amount of personal adjustment in addition to establishing the study habits that will ensure excellence in academic performance.

Any form of employment during collegiate or professional studies should be carefully selected to avoid an imbalance in time and effort between the job and academic studies. If at all possible, the student should refrain from such employment and, instead, should seek a full-time position during the summer months.

SCHOLARSHIPS AND LOANS

Funds for loans and scholarships are available and offer students a convenient means of financing a part of their education. Selecting recipients for these funds is generally based on academic records as well as genuine financial need. In most institutions, including veterinary schools, acquiring such funds during the initial year is difficult, since students must first prove their ability to cope with college work.

The type and amount of loans and scholarships vary from institution to institution. At the undergraduate level, federal and state grants are available to qualified students. Loans often may be arranged at low interest rates; many do not require repayment until after graduation. College work/study programs, which provide employment opportunities on a part-time basis, are also available. Students requiring financial help are encouraged to discuss their needs with student assistance or financial aid officers at the university.

At the veterinary schools, similar work/study programs are provided, as are loans offered under the terms of various legislative acts. Details can be obtained through the dean's office at the veterinary school.

Students should not overlook the scholarship funds provided by insurance companies, banks, and other lending agencies. These funds may be an excellent source of support, but their interest rates may not be as appealing as those loans arranged through the university.

Government Loans

The largest source of funding for veterinary medical students is government-subsidized loans. Approximately 75 percent of all students enrolled in veterinary college depend on government loans to complete their education.

There are a dizzying number of government loans available to finance a veterinary medical education. The financial aid offices at the colleges can provide students with directives on how to apply for these loans. These include Federal Perkins Loans, which are campus-based funds awarded by individual institutions. Undergraduates are eligible to borrow at least $3,000 a year up to a total of $15,000; students in veterinary colleges are considered graduate students, and are thus eligible to borrow up to $5,000 a year, as long as the combined total of undergraduate and graduate loans do not exceed $30,000. The Federal Stafford Loans are another government-subsidized source of funding for veterinary school. They allow financially eligible students to borrow up to $8,500 a year for graduate studies. Other federal student loans offer different levels of funding for higher education. The amount of financing available, however, will depend on the veterinary school at which the student is enrolled. Although the interest rates on these loans are relatively low, they nevertheless still constitute a significant financial obligation for most students. Moreover, any student who owes a refund to a federal grant program, or is in default on a federal loan, will be ineligible for further funding.

Other Available Funds

Students are also encouraged to research sources of funds in the library. Many loans or scholarships are available to students based on their ethnicity, their parents' jobs, or other unusual circumstances such as specific gifts from school alumni. Books on these loans and scholarship opportunities are available at most school, public, and college libraries.

Sometimes larger corporations are willing to help defray tuition costs for employees engaged in educational programs that will aid the company. Check with your employer and see if such an option is open to you.

Another option is a three- or four-year Army tour of duty. Upon completion of this obligation, money is available for education. It is also possible to receive some veterinary training during one's time in the military (see Chapter 8).

A good education, like all the finer things in life, is an expensive but sound investment. There are few young men and women, properly motivated, ambitious, and willing to undergo certain sacrifices, who have failed to complete veterinary education because of their lack of ability to meet the necessary financial obligations. Nevertheless, financing a veterinary education is costly; the average amount of debt by veterinary graduates is $40,000.

CONTINUING EDUCATION AND GRADUATE STUDIES

The nature and scope of veterinary responsibilities and services are constantly changing; hence, the curriculum also must change. The present four-year professional curriculum provides the fundamental foundations upon which all veterinary medicine is based. The graduate veterinarian has been adequately introduced to all the facets of modern veterinary medicine, but without the depth of understanding or proficiency in all the disciplines studied.

Internships

While medical education requires an internship as a prerequisite to a license to practice, at present no such requirement is demanded by the veterinary profession. However, there are many internships and residency programs available for the veterinary graduate who wishes to gain additional expertise in the field. These programs provide an excellent opportunity for students to add to their clinical skills or achieve additional qualification or certification in a veterinary specialty.

In addition to on-the-job internship training for better services and development of clinical specialties, these veterinarians as well as those in other fields of veterinary medicine participate in continuing education in three ways: personal reading, local seminars or conferences, and concentrated sessions lasting from a day or two to several weeks. The latter two opportunities for continuing education usually are offered by veterinary associations, or in short courses at colleges of veterinary medicine or in departments of veterinary science at the land-grant institutions. Pharmaceutical firms also contribute to and sponsor professional symposia.

Specific Programs

Each issue of the *Journal of the American Veterinary Medical Association* lists announcements of forthcoming course opportunities for veterinarians. Fields in which courses are offered include: laboratory diagnostic methods, reproductive physiology, toxicology, radiology, orthopedics, nutrition, tropical veterinary medicine, cardiology, equine diseases, biomedical engineering, dairy herd health, and many others. In some instances, the extension services of the land-grant institutions assist with programs particularly designed for the rural practitioner.

While a major share of the financial assistance has been obtained through grants from the American Veterinary Medical Association (AVMA), the National Institutes of Health (NIH), and the National Science Foundation (NSF), considerable support has also been received from industry and private foundations. Those who wish to continue their education under such programs usually receive part-time teaching appointments at the colleges, with the privilege of carrying on thesis research.

Agencies of the federal government, veterinary science departments at the land-grant institutions, and private research organizations also have developed training programs leading to advanced degrees in many of the veterinary disciplines. Information regarding specific postdoctoral programs may be obtained from the deans of the respective veterinary colleges.

CHAPTER 4

THE VETERINARIAN IN THE TWENTY-FIRST CENTURY

While veterinarians in the past were called upon to provide a range of care to a wide variety of species, veterinarians today are more likely to focus their energies in a particular field of veterinary medicine. According to a 1997 survey by the American Veterinary Medical Association, 45,200 veterinarians are involved in private clinical practice. Of these, 58 percent of veterinarians (26,235) treat small animals exclusively, while another 12.6 percent (5,717) have a practice that is predominant in small animals. Another 8.6 percent of veterinarians (3,876) in private practice treat a clientele that is predominant in large animals, and 4.2 percent (1,894) focus solely on large animals. This does not include the 4.1 percent of veterinarians (1,851) who concentrate on horses and other equids in their private practice, or the 7.6 percent (3,418) whose patient base is characterized as "mixed animal." Finally, another 4.9 percent (2,209) treat animals listed in the "other" category, including veterinarians who provide contract services to zoological parks and other organizations.

In the world of public and corporate employment for veterinarians, the statistics reveal another level of diversity. There are 10,180 veterinarians working for the government or other corporate organizations. The largest number of these veterinarians, 45.4 percent or 4,618, work for colleges and universities. Another 15.4 percent (1,570) are employed in a variety of roles in industry, 10.5 percent (1,072) work for the federal government, and 7.3 percent (740) work for state or local governments. The uniformed services of the United States is home to another 4.2 percent (428), while a large number, some 17.2 percent (1,752), are listed as working for "other" organizations.

Just as veterinarians can choose to focus on one particular species, they also can specialize in a particular area of veterinary medicine. There are currently twenty specialty areas. Veterinary specialties include: anesthesiology; behavior; dentistry; dermatology; emergency and critical care; internal medicine, including cardiology, neurology, and oncology; laboratory animal medicine; microbiology; nutrition; ophthalmology; pathology; pharmacology; poultry; specialized practices, including avian, beef cattle, canine and feline, dairy, equine, feline exclusive, food animal, and swine health management; preventive medicine (including epidemiology); radiology (including radiation oncology); surgery; theriogenology (animal reproduction); toxicology; and zoological medicine. Of the more than six thousand veterinary specialists, the largest numbers are to be found in the fields of pathology and internal medicine. The fewest specialists work in the area of radiation oncology and zoological medicine, a specialty practiced by only thirty-nine certified specialists in 1999.

To be recognized as a veterinary specialist by the AVMA, one must be a graduate veterinarian who has successfully completed the process of board certification in an AVMA specialty board or college. This requires extensive postgraduate training and experience, as well as taking and passing special examinations and a review of one's credentials.

GENERAL PRACTITIONERS

What are the responsibilities of general practitioners? One often thinks of general practitioners as working primarily with efforts to the care of livestock. Indeed, for most of the twentieth century, veterinarians directed their efforts almost exclusively to the care of cattle, sheep, and other species of special importance to the livestock industry. During the course of time, however, these veterinarians found that other services were being demanded by dog, cat, and other pet owners in the communities in which they lived. As trends in large-animal practice also began to change, general practitioners found that they could profit by assuming this additional service.

Located in the thousands of small communities throughout the country, general practitioners, above all others in the profession, must be informed and proficient in diversified skills requiring exceptional depth and breadth of knowledge.

They must realize their obligations to a vast national economy and, at the same time, assume responsibility when called upon to care for the family pet.

Regardless of the area in which one becomes established and the local predominance of any one particular livestock species, the primary responsibility of the large-animal practitioner is that of keeping animals healthy. Routine vaccination for the prevention of infectious diseases; educational conferences with livestock owners to establish disease control procedures; and advising on management practices and on feeding, breeding, and housing of animals are all in a day's work for practitioners. In addition, of course, practitioners must employ their training to recognize, diagnose, and treat individuals and groups of animals.

Purpose of Practitioners

Today's practitioners must work closely with their clients and encourage disease prevention, rather than treatment after disease has already occurred. Regularly scheduled physical examinations are necessary to recognize danger spots early and to institute corrective measures before damage is irreparable.

Veterinarians must keep the economic value of the animal in mind at all times. Sometimes it is possible to save an animal, but the cost of doing so may be too expensive for the farmer or even the pet owner. Whether caring for dairy cattle, horses, swine, sheep, goats, or any livestock, the veterinarian's responsibility remains the same—sound advice and skillful care in the maintenance of health. No longer are large-animal practitioners limited to the treatment of the sick animal as was the case only a few years ago. Veterinarians are now partners in a tremendous agricultural business.

Livestock

Changes in livestock production have a direct effect on the work of large-animal practitioners. With the increase in human populations and the rising demand for meat, milk, and other animal-source foods for human consumption, larger and more efficient specialized livestock units have been developed. The introduction of labor-saving devices has produced more milk with less work. Swine are being raised on farms where facilities will permit the production of thousands of animals per year. Feedlots where several thousand beef cattle can be fattened for commercial meat production are replacing small feeder operations.

With these innovations, livestock production requires added efficiency to balance the narrow margin of profit. Efficiency is acquired only through careful consideration and management of the operation. Veterinary medicine becomes a very important part of this process. Veterinarians must know how much it costs to lose a certain percentage of the calf or pig crop, the cost of rebreeding a cow with low reproductive capacities, the cost of feeding steers in light of the return they bring when they reach the packing house, and many other economic factors that are a part of the total productive efficiency. Veterinarians must use their knowledge of poor animal health to supplement the efforts of the herd managers and other livestock specialists.

To recent graduates, the period between graduation and a moderate degree of success in practice can be filled with frustration and discouragement. Very often they no longer have ready access to the modern facilities and equipment at the clinics of the veterinary colleges. Limited financial resources may turn them, unfortunately, to a makeshift practice. However, there are a number of options available.

CONTRACT PRACTICE

Changes in livestock production methods and the growing importance of veterinarians in agribusiness have prompted some veterinarians to use a contract practice. Since veterinarians are regarded as members of the production team in their capacity to oversee the herd health, they may now be employed by owners of these large livestock units to take full responsibility for a systematic approach to disease prevention, including routine blood testing, tuberculosis testing, parasite control, and vaccination against infectious diseases, in addition to herd examinations at periodic intervals. Through a pre-arrangement between owners and veterinarians, veterinarians are contracted to supply all these and perhaps other specific services over a particular period of time at a definite fee to include all professional assistance rendered.

This type of arrangement, which can be applied to any type of livestock operation, places the owner in a position to obtain preventive rather than strictly therapeutic veterinary medicine at a set cost to be budgeted into the entire business operation for the year. Veterinarians, on the other hand, are allowed flexibility in their services since they have full command of the entire herd-health program and are not confined to undesirable "rescue-the-perishing" emergency problems.

PARTNERSHIP PRACTICE

Another trend in veterinary medicine has been toward partnership practices. Most practices today are operated by more than one person under a variety of working arrangements. Individual practitioners are frequently overburdened. Finding the time and energy to meet the increased demands for service that are placed on them is difficult. Established practitioners may engage a second or even third person, often a recent graduate, to become a salaried "partner" in the practice. These "partners," under contract for specific periods of time, have an option to renew their contracts, to resign in favor of forming individual practices, or to assume another position.

The "partner-intern" in an established practice is provided with an excellent environment in which to work, the opportunity to gain valuable experience, and a practical means of accumulating assets needed to eventually form his or her own practice.

Financial Possibilities

A true partnership involves a financial investment by all parties concerned and an equitable distribution of profits. The specific arrangements may be varied and peculiar to a particular situation. Obviously, the outlay for such a type of practice must be carefully weighed against the income that two or three persons might expect from their services. However, the dividends in a partnership practice cannot all be measured in terms of income. More time to spend on vocational interests, being able to consult with colleagues who are close by, the satisfaction of rendering greater and more diversified service, and the opportunity to develop professional skills or engage in practical research are important considerations, too.

GROUP PRACTICE

Group practices, which expand on the partnership idea, are becoming more common across the country. In this type of practice, veterinarians within a certain area continue to conduct their individual practices. However, they also form a cooperative arrangement through which they can construct clinical facilities for common use and employ personnel for business management and laboratory assistance for common service at considerable savings in overhead. In a group practice, the several veterinarians involved may coordinate their particular professional skills and knowledge for the purpose of providing the finest type of complete professional service to the community—a service that cannot be met through the efforts of an individual veterinarian.

The drawbacks of a partnership practice include the possibilities of personality conflict or misunderstandings regarding common expenses and division of income. Those who intend to engage in such a practice must be fully aware of the legal, technical, and professional ramifications.

SPECIALTY PRACTICES

The type of practice that veterinarians choose depends on several factors: the veterinarians' backgrounds (for example, growing up on a farm around large animals), interests in veterinary school, and the geographical location of a potential practice.

For young veterinarians who were born and raised on a dairy farm, the problems surrounding the care and management of the dairy cow may hold a particular interest and lead to special studies in veterinary college. After graduating from veterinary school, they may locate in an area where dairy cattle are the main source of agricultural income. Through daily experience and study in their own practice, or preferably under the guidance of a seasoned dairy practitioner, new veterinarians soon become adept in all phases of dairy cattle production.

Short courses, conferences, and extension-service programs enhance new veterinarians' knowledge of the care of dairy cattle. Similarly, in the case of swine, cattle, sheep, poultry, and horses, experienced practitioners who specialize in one species are becoming more common and build up a practice more quickly. Further specialization, similar to that in human medicine, is also increasing, especially in larger practices.

Equestrian Veterinarians

During the past few years, there has been a steady increase in the breeding, management, and training of horses for both business and pleasure. Due to the value of these animals and the particular functions assigned to them, owners seek out veterinarians who have unusual skill and knowledge about horses. A 1998 survey by the USDA found, in fact, that 84.1 percent of equid-focused operations rated veterinarians as the most important source of information for equine health decisions. These equestrian veterinarians are among the best paid of all veterinarians.

While horses suffer from many of the same conditions of ill health as do other species of animals, they are also quite prone to unique breeding problems and digestive disorders. Injuries to the legs of racehorses can produce very serious effects on the primary function and usefulness of the animal.

Many equine practitioners work on a contract basis serving a particular stud farm. Other veterinarians are directly employed by the track or the racing commission to enforce regulations that govern horse racing. They are primarily responsible for certifying the health of the entries in each race and overseeing all the activities before, during, and after the race. These veterinarians receive salaries rather than the fixed fees usually charged by veterinary practitioners.

THE VETERINARY HOSPITAL

The veterinary hospital is an expected part of a community, and veterinarians are respected members of that community. They serve a clientele that demands only the best for the family dog, cat, canary, rabbit, and a host of other domesticated animals.

Modern clinics and hospitals, established and maintained by small-animal practitioners, offer facilities in which the veterinarian can provide the finest medical and surgical care which, in many ways, is comparable to that available for the practice of human medicine. Animal hospitals in certain cities, such as Angell Memorial Hospital in Boston and the Animal Medical Center in New York, which treats more than sixty thousand animals a year, are fine, large-scale veterinary medical centers. They are well equipped with instrumentation and kennels and staffed by trained personnel to cope with all health problems affecting small animals.

The size of the veterinary hospital will, of course, vary with the location and with the services veterinarians expect to provide. Minimal requirements will include a waiting room, office, examining room including X ray, surgery, a small laboratory, and kennel facilities for observation and postsurgical cases.

Practitioners have a responsibility to locate a veterinary hospital in an area where it will not become a nuisance from odor or noise. If possible, it should blend aesthetically with its surroundings since it is an integral part of the community.

SMALL-ANIMAL PRACTICE

The latest emphasis in veterinary practice is on a small-animal practice. As of 1997, 31.6 percent of American households owned dogs, averaging 1.69 dogs per dog-owning household. And 27.3 percent of American households owned an average of 2.19 pet cats.

The increasing number of urban and suburban households with pets has prompted new veterinarians to enter small-animal practice. Even veterinarians in rural areas have begun to assume responsibility for the care of small animals; mixed practices are also becoming more common.

Business Responsibilities

In addition to professional duties of the care of animal patients, small-animal practitioners are also businesspeople. Veterinarians must interact with the owners of animals, people who often are upset and may be unreasonable. In addition to the professional aspects of the career and the public relations side, which may be less than pleasant, there are the management concerns: billing, custodial work, payrolls, and taxes. Too often, new practitioners forget that a private practice is more than simply caring for animals—it is a business and must be run on business principles if they are to stay in business.

Categories of Work

The work of small-animal practitioners can be divided into three general categories: (1) medical treatment, (2) surgery, and (3) consultation. Medical care is further defined as outpatient and inpatient. Generally, veterinarians reserve four to six hours of the day for the care of the outpatient—the animal that can be examined, treated, and returned to the owner immediately. This care may include routine vaccinations for rabies, distemper, hepatitis, a case of mange, the treatment of minor injury, and other conditions that do not require hospitalization of the animal. On the other hand, animals suffering from severe injuries, requiring surgery, or needing further examination to furnish a diagnosis will be hospitalized or become inpatients. These animals are checked hour by hour, treatment is prescribed and administered, laboratory examinations are conducted, and other necessary services are provided.

In a small-animal practice of any size, two or three hours of the day must be spent in the performance of surgical procedures. Operations, such as spaying, setting a bone fracture, removal of a tumor, extirpation of the anal glands, and cesarean section of a pregnant animal, are among the most common surgical problems.

Small-animal practitioners also devote much of their time to the education of their clients. Owners will consult their veterinarian on the proper diet for the young puppy, the care of a pregnant cat, the grooming and personal cleanliness of a family pet, the housebreaking of newborns, and the elimination of other undesirable habits of an animal. Many owners seek advice on a long-range preventive medicine program to ensure continued health of their animals.

ZOO VETERINARIANS

Veterinarians are needed for the care of animals in the approximately 150 zoological gardens in this country. The primary job of zoo veterinarians is the clinical care of exotic or foreign animals. The disease problems, surgical procedures, and treatment of zoo animals are similar, in many respects, to those of domesticated livestock and pets. However, importation of these animals and the change from a free-living environment to one of confinement creates particular problems, such as the introduction of animal diseases not common to this country. Also, wild animals that have not had exposure to human diseases are extremely susceptible to tuberculosis, the common cold, and other respiratory diseases when placed in close contact with zoo visitors. Thus, zoo veterinarians are responsible for a program of preventive medicine directed toward the control of diseases common to humans and animals, as well as special problems in the breeding of animals in captivity and in the formulation of balanced diets.

Not very many veterinarians are employed exclusively by zoos, although positions do exist at the larger parks, such as the National Zoo in Washington, DC. Most zoo vets, however, are private practitioners who have a contract with the zoo to provide care to the captive animals. These contracts are usually for part-time jobs.

EXPECTED INCOME

In 1999 about 4.2 percent of all veterinarians were exclusively engaged in large-animal practice, which does not include the equine practitioners who make up 4.1 percent of all veterinarians. The investment in a large-animal practice is considerably lower than that necessary for the establishment of a mixed- or small-animal practice. Large-animal practitioners, however, do need to initially equip their practice with an automobile, drugs and instruments, two-way radio, X ray, and laboratory equipment. Many operate their practice out of their home or from a modest office with a minimum of investment or overhead. As the practice expands, a large-animal hospital, staffed by additional professional assistants, may become essential in order to provide the services expected by the clientele.

With current inflationary costs, it would be difficult to estimate the capital required for establishing a practice, which could range from $75,000 upward depending on the desires of the individual veterinarian and the nature of the practice.

Income Differentials

The mean individual income before taxes of experienced large-animal practitioners in an agricultural area is slightly over $76,000. The gross income is much larger, but about half is consumed by overhead.

Young veterinarian assistants in established practices are salaried employees. They receive annual salary increments depending on their success in adjusting to the business, their public relations skills and those of the practice as a whole, and their development of professional and often specialized skills. In general, specialized large-animal practices usually provide larger incomes.

The small-animal practitioner requires physical facilities and auxiliary personnel far in excess of that needed to operate a large-animal practice. Modern hospitals, well equipped and expertly staffed, are absolutely essential to provide the standard of care that the small-animal owner expects and demands. The partnership or group practice will obviously minimize what may seem to be an almost insurmountable financial obstacle for one individual.

A 1998 survey by the American Veterinary Medicine Association looked at the salaries of veterinary college graduates in their first year of employment. The study revealed a wide income differential, depending on place of employment. For example, first-year graduates in private clinical practice exclusively dedicated to the treatment of small animals earned a mean salary of $37,594. Those who worked exclusively with large animals earned a mean first-year salary of $36,724; in equine practices, the recent graduate earned just over $29,000. Salaries for veterinarians in the public and corporate spheres earned widely divergent salaries. The highest salary was paid to those serving in the military, who earned $43,533; on the other hand, new veterinarians working for universities earned a mean salary of $17,500.

The numbers for more experienced veterinarians show a similar income discrepancy. In 1997 the mean individual income for all veterinarians in private practice was $65,208; veterinarians employed by large animal exclusive practices earned about $76,360, and equine practitioners earned a mean salary of $76,089. Veterinarians who treated small animals exclusively earned a mean salary of $67,562 in 1997. The most highly paid veterinarians are those who are employed by industry; in 1997 their salary averaged about $109,941. The salaries of military veterinarians, while relatively high for first-year graduates, do not keep pace with other fields; in 1997 the average salary for military veterinarians was $60,097. This is partially due to the fact that the military veterinarian tends to be a younger professional, who often leaves the uniformed services and enters private practice after serving out his or her commitment. The average salary for veterinarians employed by the federal government was $68,153 in 1997.

A LICENSE TO PRACTICE

A license is required to practice veterinary medicine in the United States and Canada. In the United States, licensing is controlled by each state. All fifty states and the District of Columbia require that veterinarians have completed the D.V.M. degree and passed a national board examination.

Licensure examinations are given by each State Veterinary Medical Examining Board (including the District of Columbia, Puerto Rico, and Guam). The membership of the board is usually selected by the governor from the outstanding practitioners in each state. The board operating under the Veterinary Practice Act of the particular state establishes the time and place of the examination, the academic and character qualifications of the candidate, the nature of the examination material, fees to be charged for examination and annual licensure, and other pertinent matters. The examination, composed of written, oral, and practical sections, needs to be taken only once, but licenses generally must be renewed annually. Continuing education is required for relicensure in thirty-nine states, plus Puerto Rico and the District of Columbia. This requirement ranges from four to twenty credit hours. While most states require an annual renewal of a license, the trend is toward a two-year cycle. Iowa and Puerto Rico license their veterinarians for three years. In 1950 the National Board of Veterinary Medical Examiners was established to provide a comprehensive examination acceptable to all state boards or other examining agencies. This examination, prepared by the Professional Examination Service of the American Public Health Association and the National Board, is currently given in June each year.

FOREIGN VETERINARY GRADUATES

Veterinarians who were trained outside the United States can receive a license to work in this country. The Educational Commission for Foreign Veterinary Graduates (ECFVG) certifies individuals who demonstrate that they meet clinical and language proficiency requirements. The ECFVG certification satisfies the educational requirement for licensure in all states except Nebraska. Candidates must still fulfill any specific state licensing requirements to receive a license to practice in a given state.

CHAPTER 5

VETERINARIANS IN PUBLIC SERVICE

The U.S. government employs more than twenty-five hundred veterinarians. The majority work for the U.S. Department of Agriculture; others work for the Centers for Disease Control (CDC), the Food and Drug Administration (FDA) Division of Veterinary Medicine, the National Institutes of Health (NIH), and the armed services, as well as other agencies that use laboratory animals.

Veterinarians in public service also include those who work for the U.S. Fish and Wildlife Service, and the Environmental Protection Agency.

UNITED STATES DEPARTMENT OF AGRICULTURE

At least three branches of the U.S. Department of Agriculture (USDA) require the services of veterinarians. These include: the Agricultural Research Service (ARS); the Animal and Plant Health Inspection Service (APHIS); and the Food Safety and Inspection Service (FSIS).

The Agricultural Research Service

The Agricultural Research Service (ARS) administers a national program of fundamental and applied research on diseases and parasites that affect animals, poultry, and fur-bearing mammals. It is also responsible for the development of improved diagnostic agents, vaccines, and other methods for the control and eradication of diseases. In addition to infectious diseases, which become particularly devastating when protective measures are relaxed, nutritional diseases, poisonings, and other conditions associated with livestock and poultry management also receive attention.

Veterinarians and other scientists in related disciplines, such as bacteriology, virology, mycology, and pathology, work in teams to reach the solution to problems of regional, national, or international importance. The research results are disseminated throughout the country and the world. In many instances, these scientific discoveries, initially aimed at animal health, have a direct bearing on human health and welfare.

ARS Laboratories

The work of the ARS is concentrated at four main laboratories, located at Beltsville, Maryland; Plum Island, New York; Ames, Iowa; and College Station, Texas. In addition, there are smaller field laboratories in other parts of the United States.

The Plum Island laboratory directs its primary attention to the diagnosis, prevention, control, and eradication of communicable foreign diseases that may be of potential danger to this country. The National Veterinary Services Laboratories at the Ames laboratory, on the other hand, are concerned with the study of communicable domestic diseases. Personnel are trained in pathology, parasitology, microbiology, virology, serology, and immunology. Beltsville research is aimed toward animal parasites. At College Station, the toxicological and pathological effects of chemicals used in controlling livestock and plant pests are under study.

Scientists engaged in ARS research programs have gained worldwide acclaim for their outstanding contributions to veterinary medicine. For the young veterinarian seeking a career in research, particularly fine opportunities exist in the ARS.

Animal and Plant Health Inspection Service

The veterinarians who work for APHIS play a critical role in protecting the health and marketability of America's animals. They practice veterinary medicine on a large scale, dealing with animal health problems of local, regional, national, and even international importance. APHIS veterinarians also have the opportunity to provide valuable one-on-one support to livestock and poultry producers in the prevention and control of disease.

SPECIFIC FUNCTIONS

The veterinarians working for the agency also play a role in several other ways, including:

1. The control and eradication of outbreaks of diseases of economic importance among animals and poultry in the United States.

2. The protection of U.S. livestock and poultry from diseases of foreign origin through inspection and quarantine at air and sea points of entry and the rejection of disease-carrying animals.

3. The control and eradication of disease outbreaks of foreign origin that may have escaped our border defenses. Costly experiences in the past have taught American veterinarians that inspection and quarantine are profitable procedures. Uncontrolled diseases to which American livestock and poultry are particularly susceptible are found throughout the world, and jet-age transportation permits the possible entry of animals with disease at an undetectable stage of development. Without an alert protective system supported by diagnosticians, epidemiologists, management specialists, laboratory workers, and others, contamination of our domestic stock could be disastrous. Enforcement of domestic and international regulations to prevent, control, and eradicate diseases of either internal or external origin is a vital function of the USDA.

4. Certification of the disease-free status of animals and animal products destined for export. This ensures that the American producer and processor markets a quality product that will compete favorably on the world market and will not endanger the health of animal and human populations in the importing countries.

5. The control of biological materials prepared for animal use to ensure their purity, potency, safety, and effectiveness. Veterinarians are concerned with the licensing, evaluation, and handling of products shipped or sold interstate.

6. Enforcement of the Horse Protection Act, which protects horses against painful and inhumane methods in management, and the Animal Welfare Act, which protects animals in zoos and circuses and also ensures adequate standards of care for housing, watering, sanitation, veterinary care, and human handling for animals sold as pets at the wholesale level or used for research or exhibition.

In 1993 the Animal Welfare Act was amended to help prevent the use of lost and stolen pets in research. Under APHIS supervision, the amendment requires that animal shelters hold dogs and cats for at least five days before releasing them to the dealers who provide animal subjects to research laboratories.

A broad array of nontraditional fields is also available to the veterinarian working for APHIS. These include epidemiology, computerized disease surveillance, biotechnology, and educational support for producers.

The Food Safety and Inspection Service

The FSIS is responsible for the protection of the American consumer through inspection of food products of animal origin, ensuring their sanitary handling, wholesomeness, and accurate labeling. All meat and meat products processed in the United States for interstate or foreign shipment must be federally inspected. About 80 percent of all animals slaughtered annually are so inspected; the remainder fall under state or municipal jurisdiction for inspection.

WHAT FSIS VETERINARIANS DO

Approximately 1,400 veterinarians (including state and industrial veterinarians) are employed in the inspection of more than 130 million meat animals and 3 billion birds slaughtered yearly at 6,000 processing plants throughout the country. This work is covered by various laws, including the Poultry Inspection Act of 1957 requiring inspection of all poultry sold in interstate commerce, and the 1996 Hazard Analysis and Critical Control Point (HACCP) rules, which regulate pathogens (harmful bacteria) in meat and poultry. FSIS veterinarians also are responsible for the certification of more than 1,000 plants in 45 foreign countries that ship meat products to the United States.

The FSIS has more than 1,200 veterinarians on staff, the largest group of veterinarians within a USDA department, and they hire between 90 and 120 veterinarians each year.

USDA Income Grades

Veterinary positions with the USDA—ARS, APHIS, and FSIS—are filled by the Office of Personnel Management. Salaries for veterinarians range from the GS-9 base salary of $34,575 to the GS-12 base salary of $50,139.

Those entering APHIS are given almost a year of training in various phases of APHIS's operations before they are assigned to their permanent position. This enables the trainees to decide whether they will be happy with a career at APHIS. Though the APHIS operation is not increasing in scope, a large number of personnel are slated for retirement; so employment options are available at this agency.

U.S. PUBLIC HEALTH SERVICE

The recognition of the importance of veterinary services concerned with problems common to both humans and animals has only evolved since World War II. Except for the fine efforts of a few veterinarians in milk sanitation, food handling, and insect and rodent control programs during World War I and the outstanding contributions of veterinary parasitologists in the Public Health Service, little opportunity was afforded members of the veterinary profession to demonstrate their capabilities to cooperate with the medical profession in studies related to human health.

At the end of World War II, however, a veterinary public health program was established to meet the needs of the nation, and a veterinary category was created as a distinct professional group within the military service. As a result, the second half of the twentieth century saw tremendous growth and diversity in the activities of veterinary public health on the national, state, and local levels.

Contributions and Responsibilities

Veterinary contributions to the public health have been numerous. Concepts already well established about the health of animals are frequently adapted and implemented in the attack on human diseases. Many drugs used with animals have gone on to prove effective treatments for human ailments such as arthritis. Veterinary public health protects and advances human health by using the combined knowledge of the interrelationships of animal and human health.

Veterinary officers in the Public Health Service participate in a great variety of assignments, including the control and eradication of zoonoses; the development and supervision of food sanitation; laboratory and research projects in diagnosis, biologics production, zootechnics96, microbiology, epidemiology, comparative medicine, and pathology; and the education and training of professional workers in veterinary aspects of public health.

Research projects cover such studies as parasite populations in laboratory animals, the comparative pathology of various animal species, cardiovascular diseases in people and animals, cancer, and the development of improved techniques for the prompt and accurate diagnosis of disease. Training courses in laboratory and field procedures, preparation of educational pamphlets and audiovisual aids, and other activities are conducted by veterinary public health training officers. State and local public health departments also use the resources of the Public Health Service.

AFFILIATED FEDERAL AGENCIES

Most of the activities of the veterinarians in public health work are directly associated with the NIH in Washington, DC, and the CDC in Atlanta, Georgia. In 1999 there were forty-seven full-time professionals with the D.V.M. degree working at the NIH. Along with veterinarians at the CDC, the NIH veterinarians study comparative parasitology, pathology, and anatomy of laboratory animals used for experimental purposes, and management and nutritional requirements of these animals. Veterinarians are also working on research teams with members of other professions in the study of heart disease, cancer, arthritis, and other problems common to animal and human populations.

COMMUNICABLE DISEASE RESEARCH

At the Public Health Service Communicable Disease Laboratory, comprehensive nationwide programs for the prevention and control of communicable diseases are developed.

Research at this laboratory includes studies on the cause of disease, pathogenesis, host-parasite relationships, and the treatment of such representative diseases as encephalitis, rabies, food poisoning, anthrax, leptospirosis, parasitic diseases among all species of animals, and many other diseases of importance to both livestock and human populations.

Each year, substantial funds are appropriated by Congress and administered by the NIH to support a wide variety of health-related research projects conducted by scientists attached to a number of institutions outside the Public Health Service. While these projects are veterinary in nature, they have considerable significance for the health of the nation. Examples include comparative cardiovascular studies, zoonoses research, and research on the aging process. The programs, projects, and responsibilities of the U.S. Public Health Service and its affiliated institutions provide excellent opportunities for future veterinarians.

EDUCATIONAL REQUIREMENTS

The basic educational requirement for appointment to the U.S. Public Health Service is the degree of Doctor of Veterinary Medicine. However, many veterinary officers hold advanced degrees in veterinary public health, or in a particular specialty such as pathology or parasitology. Practical field work in disease control and eradication is beneficial. Veterinarians may enter the Public Health Service either by direct appointment to the Commissioned Corps or through the Office of

Personnel Management. The Commissioned Corps officers hold rank and draw pay similar to military officers. They are generally commissioned in the rank of Senior Assistant Veterinarian, comparable to a captain in the military service.

UNITED STATES FOOD AND DRUG ADMINISTRATION

The Bureau of Veterinary Medicine of the FDA is a branch of the Public Health Service. It is responsible for the safety and efficacy of drugs, antibiotics, and medicated feeds used in livestock and poultry. Products must be processed under specifications that include accurate labeling of contents and use. The bureau reviews the experimental evidence that indicates that the product has no harmful effects on the animal body and that no residual material remains in the animal body that could be detrimental to the consumer of the processed meats or their by-products.

Evaluation of Drugs

The effectiveness of consumer protection depends largely on voluntary compliance with drug-use recommendations. Proper use is encouraged and supported through the educational activities of the bureau in cooperation with field veterinarians and extension workers. The bureau's research branch conducts studies that evaluate the validity of the manufacturer's data on the safety and efficacy of the drugs. These veterinarians are key individuals in safeguarding animals, their owners, and the general public against unscrupulous and careless practices in the uses of drugs and other chemical agents.

The classification of FDA veterinarians is similar to those employed in the USDA with comparable salaries and fringe benefits.

PUBLIC SERVICE AT THE STATE AND LOCAL LEVELS

One of the basic veterinary functions of the USDA is the prevention of the introduction of foreign diseases into the country. Further, if these diseases do gain entrance, controls are imposed by the federal government as quickly as possible.

In the control and eradication of both foreign and indigenous diseases, the USDA, in association with state commissioners and secretaries of agriculture, has developed policies to guide cooperative federal-state efforts. The federal government works with the states to reduce or eliminate losses caused by particular diseases and to prevent the interstate spread of diseases.

Responsible State Agencies

The states have the responsibility of protecting their own livestock producers and working closely with them and practicing veterinarians in controlling localized diseases. They also cooperate with the federal government when serious outbreaks of disease occur and are in danger of spreading beyond the geographical limits of a particular state.

Each of the fifty states has an agency responsible for the health of animals within its jurisdiction. This agency is directed by a state veterinarian who supervises the various activities of other veterinarians on the staff. Generally, the disease-control responsibilities are concerned with tuberculosis, brucellosis, scabies, hog cholera, pullorum diseases, rabies, and other diseases that pose a threat to the state's livestock industry or to human health. In most cases, the services and cooperation of the ARS, the APHIS, and the practicing veterinarian are used in these programs.

In addition, the states supervise the interstate and intrastate movement of livestock; enforce quarantines on premises harboring infected animals and poultry; maintain diagnostic laboratories to assist veterinarians and livestock owners in making accurate decisions on the nature, control, and treatment of specific diseases; and license and supervise livestock exhibits.

In many states, the animal disease agencies are also responsible for meat inspection in packing houses not under federal supervision. These veterinary responsibilities are identical to those in federally inspected packing plants. The state animal disease-control agency is a vital link in the fight against animal disease. These agencies offer many opportunities for public service. Compensation in many states is equal to that in similar positions in the USDA.

VETERINARIANS AS SPECIALISTS

Only in recent years have veterinary medical services been integrated into all levels of public health work. In modern health departments, veterinarians are being recognized for their specialized training and competencies. Veterinarians now serve as consultants to state, municipal, and county health departments in communicable disease control, food hygiene, laboratory diagnosis, and epidemiological studies.

As local, county, and state health departments expand and share more of the responsibilities of the U.S. Public Health Service, the scope of work necessitating veterinary "know-how" will also increase. Veterinary medicine will play a greater role in public health programs since the veterinarian is now a most-needed member of a multidisciplinary approach to the solution of public health problems.

VETERINARIANS IN WORLD SERVICE

The emergence of new nations has created world problems more deeply rooted than those of a purely political nature. The fate of these countries lies principally in their ability to produce food supplies of adequate quantity and quality to meet the nutritional needs of their citizens. The development and maintenance of food products of animal origin; the health of livestock for use as sources of power; the control of animal factors in soil fertility for crop production; and the production of leather, wool, and other fibers for clothing are basic requirements for sustenance and economic survival.

All the new nations face serious shortages in veterinary services, particularly in the control of livestock diseases. Modern transportation systems may carry destructive diseases from one country to another. Few countries have facilities for training their own people in disease control and in the great variety of existing veterinary services. Embryonic institutions are appearing in several of these countries but much of their support, both in funds and personnel, must come from countries where veterinary medicine is well established and where financial and technical assistance can be offered.

The problems are particularly crucial in the African and the Southeast Asian countries. In the vast area of West Africa, the veterinarian-livestock ratio is about 1:1,000,000, compared to about 1:200,000 in the United States. Disease control and productive livestock management are likely to break down completely under such conditions, in addition to the probable effect of many of these diseases on the people of these countries. Uncontrolled animal diseases invariably lead to serious human health problems.

PROVIDING ASSISTANCE ABROAD

The United States provides vast sums of money to emerging nations to aid in raising their living standards. Unfortunately, the importance of animal health has only been partially appreciated by the U.S. government, by private philanthropic agencies, and by a number of other countries. At best, the problem of foreign technical aid is difficult. Few qualified veterinarians are willing or able to spend more than a short period of time in foreign service. Working with veterinary counterparts and government officials in other countries may lead to a sense of failure or lack of accomplishment.

A new approach must be developed in each country to provide the type of service that will be most beneficial for that country in the shortest period of time. Veterinarians who desire to serve the human and livestock needs of a foreign nation, with its own cultural and social traditions, must possess a sincere humanitarian spirit. Patience, adaptiveness, ingenuity, sympathetic understanding, excellent personal health, willingness to live under adverse conditions, and a broad knowledge of the art and science of veterinary medicine are among the qualifications necessary for this career.

The participation of veterinarians in international organizations and cooperating U.S. agencies helps to promote better understanding between this nation and foreign countries. The efforts of all these agencies are directed toward the improvement of local animal resources, the exchange of technical information in disease and parasite control, and the development of educational programs to train potential veterinarians in foreign countries. Other efforts enable these countries to improve their veterinary and public health programs through the activities of veterinary advisers. The future of many of these objectives depends largely on the availability of funds.

AGENCY FOR INTERNATIONAL DEVELOPMENT

The Agency for International Development (AID) is the official technical assistance branch of the U.S. government. American veterinarians develop disease-prevention and eradication programs adapted to the conditions of the particular country, provide practical demonstrations to farmers and local veterinarians, train local personnel in the vaccination procedures for the prevention of a particular indigenous disease, assist in equipping laboratories for vaccine production, and carry out special teaching and research assignments in cooperation with local veterinary schools. American veterinarians have been responsible for improving sanitation and inspection in food processing, in improving the quality of food for local consumption, and in some instances, in increasing the export market for these products.

Veterinarians working under AID programs may be engaged directly by AID as regular employees, or they may be recruited by various land-grant colleges and universities that operate under special assistance contracts with AID.

ROLE OF THE USDA

The USDA's ARS coordinates the exchange of technical knowledge between the research and regulatory divisions in that department and government veterinarians in countries around the world. The USDA also helps train foreign veterinarians at American schools of veterinary medicine, in departments of veterinary science at the land-grant colleges, at veterinary diagnostic laboratories, or at other institutions. American veterinarians supervising such training programs are contributing to the reduction of animal diseases and the ultimate improvement in human health in the countries to which these trainees will return. The contact establishes a better understanding of the problems of the foreign country; at the same time, foreign veterinarians carry home an understanding of the United States and its people, as well as broad technical knowledge.

INTERNATIONAL COOPERATION

On the international level, the United Nations and its agencies have assumed much of the responsibility for attacking the food problems of developing countries. The Food and Agricultural Organization (FAO) aims to raise the standard of living in countries by improving nutrition; increasing efficiency of farms, forests, and fisheries; and improving rural living conditions.

This agency functions somewhat differently from AID or other institutions providing direct technical assistance. Veterinary assistance is given in several ways. At the Rome headquarters of FAO, an international team of veterinarians provides information and advice on request to member nations. Veterinarians there also serve on survey teams to study means by which certain veterinary problems may be approached.

When the World Health Organization (WHO), an arm of the United Nations, was formed in 1948, veterinary medicine was integrated into its program so veterinary public health could be implemented on a global scale. The organization provides veterinary specialists as advisers to government health agencies. It organizes international conferences to act on problems of common concern to many countries. It establishes expert committees on such problems as rabies, brucellosis, tuberculosis, leptospirosis, cardiovascular disease, cancer, parasitic diseases, and meat and milk hygiene. These committees recommend courses of action to guide WHO policy toward the coordination and promotion of research and to disseminate knowledge on technical subjects through training courses and publications. WHO works closely with FAO and other international organizations in its efforts toward control of zoonoses and the furtherance of veterinary education in the public health field.

At present, WHO veterinarians are engaged in a number of important research projects, including studies of food-borne diseases such as salmonella, and inquiries into the emergence of new zoonotic agents such as those that cause bovine spongiform encephalopathy. They are also researching viruses transmitted by birds, as well as rare but still threatening outbreaks of anthrax, monkeypox, leptospirosis, and other diseases.

INVOLVEMENT IN THE AMERICAS

The Pan American Sanitary Bureau, an arm of the Pan American Health Organization, established its veterinary medical program in 1949 and serves as the regional representative of the WHO in the Americas. Career veterinary consultants in this organization provide assistance to many countries of Central and South America. Again, because zoonoses are the center of responsibility of these veterinarians, diagnosis, biological production, prevention, and control and research are among the specific duties assigned.

THE PEACE CORPS

Since few developing countries have an adequate number of trained veterinarians, they are turning to the United States. For example, the Peace Corps annually employs about six hundred veterinarians and mature-animal technicians to engage in subsistence work in foreign countries. The animal technicians who have substantial domestic experience must be trained in animal husbandry programs, including swine and sheep care.

Further information about a Peace Corps two-year commitment is available from the U.S. Peace Corps, 1111 Twentieth Street NW, Washington, DC 20526.

CHAPTER 6

VETERINARIANS IN INDUSTRY

The role of veterinarians employed by industry encompasses a wide range of responsibilities, from overseeing the health of animals raised for food production to researching new drugs for pharmaceutical companies. Veterinarians in industrial employment are not expressly limited to caring for animals and are often involved at the managerial level, as well as in marketing and sales.

Veterinarians became noticeably active in industry following World War II, as human and veterinary pharmaceutical and biological companies began to recognize the common use of many of their drugs. Intensive research into the possibilities of treating humans with drugs previously used in animals, and vice versa, led to a series of mergers between a variety of pharmaceutical companies. Indeed, today most large companies that produce medicines for humans also have established veterinary divisions, which are critically important to the research, production, and sales of new treatments.

According to the AVMA, in 1999 there were 1,570 veterinarians employed by various industries in the United States.

Of these veterinarians, 74.7 percent were men and 25.3 percent were women. Working in industry is one of the most lucrative fields for veterinarians, with an average salary of $109,941 in 1999.

VETERINARIANS IN THE DRUG INDUSTRY

The largest number of industrial veterinarians work for the drug industry, as members of a team in the development and marketing of pharmaceuticals, antibiotics, and biologicals for the treatment, prevention, and diagnosis of disease. Unlimited opportunities lie in basic and applied research, new drug development, and production. Veterinarians are responsible for quality control, consisting of laboratory testing to determine the safety and efficacy of vaccines and drugs to be used in specific disease conditions.

The drug industry continues to strive for products with the greatest therapeutic, preventive, or diagnostic effectiveness. In this effort, the toxicity of the drug and its effect on animal tissues must be determined by veterinarians using laboratory animals. The techniques used in the development and testing of these drugs are complex and require more veterinarians trained in pathology, pharmacology, and toxicology.

With this type of specialization, veterinarians in industrial work are in constant demand and salaries are comparable to income earned in private practice. Many industrial veterinarians are key individuals in the administrative structure of the company.

VETERINARIANS IN THE FOOD INDUSTRY

The food industry is a particularly dynamic area of employment for the veterinarian. The commercial feed industry employs a significant number of veterinarians, especially those with special practical training in biochemistry and nutrition and their application to livestock management.

Many animal feeds, including pet foods, are supplemented with vitamins, minerals, and antibiotics to enhance their nutritive value, promote growth, prevent infection, and for other direct and indirect therapeutic effects. Such feeds must again be prepared and tested under veterinary supervision.

OTHER INDUSTRY OPPORTUNITIES

Veterinarians with practical experience will find opportunity in areas of technical field service, public relations, and sales. Such veterinarians are of particular value in keeping industry informed of changes occurring in livestock production and in veterinary practice that may affect research, production, and sales policies. Likewise, these veterinarians assist practicing veterinarians and livestock owners in special problems, and in doing so maintain desirable relations between producer and consumer. Veterinarians also serve as directors of diagnostic laboratories established and supported by industries to provide a more complete technical service to their customers.

The opportunities in industry are unlimited, and the diversity of its services to both veterinary and human medicine continues to enlarge. Veterinarians may find that their professional qualifications and administrative abilities place them in top management and research activities in America's businesses.

CHAPTER 7

INSTITUTIONAL TEACHING AND RESEARCH

Currently more than 6,000 academic and professional personnel (not including interns or residents) are employed in U.S. schools of veterinary medicine. Of this group, about 4,600 hold veterinary degrees, and more than 1,000 hold an earned Ph.D., either alone or in combination with the veterinary degree. In the past, academic veterinarians received salaries far lower than the average. Currently, however, the average salary for a veterinarian in academia is $75,984; the profession-wide average is about $70,000.

The preparation for institutional teaching and its related research functions is long and arduous. Recent veterinary graduates entering teaching and research are usually employed by veterinary colleges with the provision that work toward the M.S. or Ph.D. degree becomes a part of the employment agreement. The instructor will be expected to carry out some academic duties and, at the same time, complete the course and research requirements for the graduate degree within one or two years. Instructors who have attained the master's degree can ordinarily expect increases in rank and salary according to their abilities, performance, and progress in their teaching assignments and/or research projects.

To progress to top positions in teaching and research, veterinarians must attain the Ph.D. degree. A program aimed toward this degree cannot always be initiated immediately after completion of the master's degree, but generally some provision can be made to release the potentially fine teachers or researchers for further graduate work later in their academic career.

REWARDS OF ACADEMIC WORK

With the improved financial status of teachers, positions in education are more attractive than ever before. However, the advantages are not entirely related to income. Working in an academic atmosphere is both stimulating and rewarding to those who seek intellectual, as well as professional, growth. Some of the best laboratories and research facilities are located at universities. In addition, the university community provides an excellent environment for the life and education of the family. The teacher-researcher is afforded the best opportunity to make many significant contributions to the profession. Teachers are in a position to mold future veterinarians to meet the expanding responsibilities of their profession, while an individual's research program can provide knowledge that may, in a very significant manner, influence the future of veterinary and medical science.

RESEARCH AGENCIES AND CATEGORIES

Veterinary research is conducted by the USDA, the U.S. Public Health Service, the FDA, and the NIH. These groups also monitor grants given to outside groups engaging in research. A large percentage of the research dollars go to researchers at state-supported colleges of higher education. As a result of this research, hundreds of millions of dollars' worth of livestock and other animals are saved each year.

The types of veterinary research conducted by the federal government, the veterinary colleges and departments, and by industry may be classified in the areas of agriculture, biology and medicine, zoonoses, pet animals, zoo and fur-bearing animals, laboratory animals, and comparative medicine. Veterinarians in basic biological and medical research are concerned with studies on environment, space, urbanization, behavior, mental health, toxicology, radiation, marine biology, and many other rapidly developing fields requiring competencies in immunology, nutrition, pathology, microbiology, and a variety of other scientific areas.

Marine Research

Marine science is another area of veterinary concern. Eighty percent of all life is found in the sea, and sea-life management, or farming for new food resources, demands veterinarians trained in fresh- or saltwater biology. The sea offers recreational opportunities, and people spend millions of hours exploring it. Health problems associated with the sea environment are studied by physiologists and other basic science teams, including veterinarians.

LINK BETWEEN HUMAN AND ANIMAL HEALTH

Veterinary research is concerned with comparative medicine, the interrelationships between human and veterinary medicine that can provide knowledge to both professions and benefits to both animal and human welfare.

Zoonoses are those diseases that are transmissible from animals to humans through contact, food, and vectors. There are about 150 such diseases, and research is directed toward improvement of methods limiting transmission and in controlling and eradicating these diseases in the animal.

Much of the support for research in pet animals comes from private sources such as the Pet Food Institute, the pet food industry's public and media relations organization. While the research is directed primarily toward the benefit of the animal, such research frequently leads to a better understanding of physiological and pathological mechanisms in humans.

Veterinarians have long been active in bioengineering, which joins the two medicines with engineering. The development of equipment and techniques for measurement and evaluation of biological processes, for supplementing or replacing weakened tissues or organs, or for other functions requires the combined knowledge and skills of the biological and physical sciences.

Finally, animals are often better suited as subjects for the study of human disease than are humans. Few human diseases have not been challenged, brought under control, or eradicated without the use of animal research. Animals are subject to many of the same diseases or similar diseases to those affecting people, and more than 250 so-called "animal disease models" have been identified, including diabetes in dogs, gastric ulcers in swine, and anemia in horses.

THE EXTENSION VETERINARIAN

Approximately one-third of the land-grant institutions in the United States employ a total of about forty extension veterinarians. Veterinary Extension has developed within the Agriculture Extension Service, an arm of the USDA.

The primary function of these extension veterinarians is to educate agriculturalists in the control and prevention of livestock diseases. These veterinarians enlist the cooperation of practicing veterinarians, state and federal regulatory officials, other extension personnel, and professional colleagues on the instruction and research staffs of the departments of veterinary science at state universities.

Veterinary Extension is a means of informing livestock owners of the possibilities of disease prevention and of helping the practitioners work more effectively. Well-informed farmers, with the cooperation of their veterinarian, can reduce disease losses. Extension veterinarians serve to interpret the results obtained by research and make these findings available to livestock owners for practical application.

Primary Responsibilities

Extension veterinarians, assisted by practitioners and livestock officials, have assumed leadership in promoting disease-eradication programs, such as the campaigns against tuberculosis and brucellosis. Control measures in hog cholera, scrapie, parasitic infections, and many other diseases are explained to livestock owners by agricultural extension personnel after consulting with extension veterinarians. Educational programs stress preventive medicine, and greater attention is given to public health problems in agricultural communities.

Secondly, extension veterinarians cooperate with all livestock and farmers' organizations, including youth organizations, such as 4-H and Future Farmers of America (FFA), all of whom are receptive to information on livestock problems. Extension veterinarians depend on home economists to carry the information on diseases of public health importance to farm families.

Since few veterinarians are engaged in poultry practice and research, the poultry industry looks to the extension service for guidance in controlling poultry diseases. In many instances, the extension service is the only liaison between the poultry farmer and research on poultry diseases.

Academic and Communication Skills

Generally extension veterinarians use meetings, conferences, and other personal contacts to disseminate educational information and to discuss control and eradication programs. Extension veterinarians are also prolific writers. Through correspondence, newspaper and magazine releases, and participation in radio and television programs, extension agents serve as the profession's public relations agents.

Continuing education programs are conducted by veterinary associations and the veterinary colleges. Yet, in states where extension services are well developed, they also are responsible for these programs.

Since extension veterinarians are members of the academic staff at land-grant institutions, they enjoy personal and financial rewards comparable to those of veterinarians in teaching and research assignments. Extension veterinarians should have some experience in large-animal practice, must enjoy meeting and talking with livestock owners seeking information, and must be willing to spend considerable time traveling to offer the type of services demanded by the livestock interests of their state.

The veterinary profession is playing a leading part in implementation of the primary objectives of the land-grant system— to develop and integrate programs in teaching, research, and extension.

LABORATORY ANIMAL MEDICINE

Each year millions of mice, rats, rabbits, guinea pigs, monkeys, dogs, and cats are used in conducting research projects related to human and animal medicine. The controversy over the abuse of laboratory animals has prompted the American Veterinary Medical Association to take a stand. (This problem will be discussed more fully at the end of this chapter.) These animals are useful tools in the testing of drugs and chemicals prior to their release for therapeutic use in humans and other animals; in determining the effects of radioactivity on animal tissues; in studying behavioral reactions that may be related to space travel; in tracing the pathogenesis of infectious disease; and in many other problems affecting animal and human health.

Veterinarians serve as consultants to universities and colleges, commercial laboratories, and government and private research institutes that maintain animals to support research. Success in nutritional, genetic, pathological, and all forms of biological research depends largely on the availability of high quality, disease-free laboratory animals.

The procurement, management, and breeding of these animals has added another responsibility to the veterinary profession. Working as members of research teams, veterinarians aid in the planning and conduct of animal research, giving special attention to the procedures used in the humane care of these animals. Active participation in these projects includes the preparation of animals for research, surgical and clinical assistance during the course of the experimentation, and the gross and microscopic examination and evaluation of animal tissues at the termination of the project. Through training and understanding of several biological disciplines, the laboratory animal veterinarian is in an excellent position to make significant contributions to both veterinary and human medicine.

SCIENTIFIC ORGANIZATIONS

Veterinarians in laboratory animal medicine are also engaged in research aimed toward the improvement of the quality of the laboratory animals. Research and information on problems of disease diagnosis, housing, breeding, and nutrition are lacking. Interchange of information on the care and management of animal colonies is available from the Institute of Laboratory Animal Research, which is part of the National Research Council of the National Academy of Science. This organization serves as a coordinating agency and a national and international resource for compiling and disseminating information on laboratory animals. It also promotes education and the humane care of laboratory animals.

The American College of Laboratory Animal Medicine (ACLAM), a specialty board recognized by the American Veterinary Medical Association, was founded in 1957. ACLAM was established to encourage training and research in laboratory animal medicine, and to establish standards of training and experience for veterinarians in this field.

For board certification, the graduate veterinarian must have four years of experience in laboratory animal medicine; must be a member of the American Veterinary Medical Association; must have been the primary author of an original article published in a peer-reviewed journal; and must complete an examination in this specialty. Pioneering institutions in this type of training are the Walter Reed Army Institute of Research, Washington, DC; Bowman Gray School of Medicine, Winston-Salem, NC; the University of California; and the University of Michigan. Veterinary graduates with specialized training in laboratory animal medicine are currently in great demand, and it is expected that these demands will increase rapidly as animal research continues to receive more attention in the biomedical fields.

AVMA POSITIONS ON ANIMALS USED IN RESEARCH AND TEACHING

The American Veterinary Medical Association has articulated its position regarding the use of animals in research and teaching, which is as follows:

USDA/APHIS Animal Welfare Program: The AVMA encourages adequate funding for the U.S. Department of Agriculture (USDA) Animal and Plant Health Inspection Service (APHIS) programs that provide for investigation and enforcement activities to prevent cruelty and enhance the welfare of animals. The AVMA recommends that all warm-blooded animals used for nonagricultural research, testing, experimentation, or exhibition be covered under the Federal Animal Welfare Act; provided that sufficient funds are made available to the Secretary of Agriculture for adequate training of inspectors and enforcement activities.

Use of Animals in Pre-college Education: The AVMA endorses the Principles and Guidelines for the Use of Animals in Pre-college Education, as prepared by the Institute of Laboratory Animal Resources, Commission on Life Sciences, National Research Council, National Academy of Sciences. (A copy of these guidelines is available upon request from the AVMA Education and Research Division.)

Use of Animals in Research, Testing, and Education: The AVMA recognizes that animals play a central and essential role in research, testing, and education for continued improvement in the health and welfare of human beings and animals. The AVMA also recognizes that humane care of animals used in research, testing, and education is an integral part of those activities. In keeping with these concerns, the AVMA endorses the principles embodied in the "Three R" tenet of Russell and Burch (1959). These principles are: refinement of experimental methods to eliminate or reduce animal pain and distress; reduction of the number of animals consistent with sound experimental design; and replacement of animals with nonanimal methods wherever feasible. The AVMA condemns all acts of vandalism against researchers and research facilities. Such acts make it more difficult for responsible individuals and groups to work for continued improvement in research animal care and treatment. The use of animals is a privilege carrying with it unique professional, scientific, and moral obligations. The AVMA encourages proper stewardship of animals, but defends and promotes the use of animals in meaningful research, testing, and education programs.

Use of Random-Source Dogs and Cats for Teaching and Biomedical Research: The carefully controlled use of random-source animals contributes greatly to improving the health and welfare of both animals and human beings. Therefore, the AVMA believes that there is ample justification for the prudent and humane use of random-source animals in veterinary medical education and biomedical research, provided that:

1. The institution conducting such teaching and/or research has met all legal requirements and guidelines pertaining to the acquisition, care, and use of animals for these purposes;

2. The individual investigators have thoughtfully examined the need for such animals and have appropriately selected the species and carefully determined the number required to meet the needs of the protocol;

3. Adequate safeguards are used to ensure that only unidentified, unowned, and specifically authorized animals are obtained from animal shelters and humane societies for these purposes; and

4. Preventive measures are taken to guarantee the health of animals obtained from such facilities before they are used in teaching or research situations.

CHAPTER 8

VETERINARIANS IN THE MILITARY

HISTORY OF THE VETERINARY CORPS

The need for veterinarians in the U.S. military stretches back to the days of the American Revolution. In 1776 General Washington directed that a "regiment of horses with a farrier" be raised to support the military. Throughout the nineteenth century, veterinarians were employed by the Army to care for military animals. During the American Civil War, each cavalry regiment had a veterinary surgeon to care for the cavalry horses, and in 1879 Congress passed a resolution requiring all military veterinarians to be graduates of one of the recognized veterinary colleges.

Veterinarians also were employed to inspect the meat, poultry, and dairy products used by the military, as well as the supplies for frontier posts. By the beginning of the twentieth century, there was growing awareness in the United States of the importance of sanitation in food processing. In 1905 Upton Sinclair published *The Jungle,* a book detailing the unsanitary methods used in meatpacking houses. It created an uproar, drawing attention to the need for monitoring food processing. In response, the American Veterinary Medical Association, as well as many individuals, pressed for the establishment of a U.S. Army Veterinary Corps.

In 1916 the U.S. Army Veterinary Corps was formally established by an act of Congress. The Veterinary Corps is part of the regular U.S. Army. When the United States entered World War I in April 1917, there were already fifty-seven veterinarians in the Veterinary Corps, mainly involved in caring for the Army's cavalry horses. Within the next two years, the new Veterinary Corps grew to more than twenty-three hundred officers.

Another important development began to take place during the Korean and Vietnam conflicts, as military veterinary medicine moved away from a focus on horses and mules and toward military working dogs, increased food sanitation, and civic action programs in the local environments, such as helping with issues concerning herd health, vaccinations, and production advice.

Since the inception of the Army Veterinary Corps, the veterinarians of the armed services have played a significant role in maintaining the health of animals and soldiers, both at home and overseas. In the past half-century, a large number of veterinarians also have become board-certified specialists. Military veterinarians have been engaged in research that has led to many groundbreaking discoveries in the treatment of injuries and illnesses in both animals and soldiers. Indeed, developments in biomedical research, aviation, and space medicine have drawn on the talents and insights of military veterinarians.

VETCOM

The United States Army Veterinary Command (VET-COM) provides military veterinary services to the U.S. Army Medical Command (MEDCOM). VETCOM was created out of the former Directorate of Veterinary Services, U.S. Army Health Services Command. The top priority issues for VETCOM include providing animal medicine, implementing a technology-based food safety program, working to assess food bioterrorism threats, and providing expanded support to the Navy, Marines, and Air Force. VETCOM is the senior headquarters for about 35 percent of United States Army veterinarians worldwide.

DISEASE PREVENTION

Veterinarians in the military assist in programs designed to protect the health of military and civilian personnel. Sanitation, handling of food and water supplies, waste disposal, insect and rodent control, and other systems are of concern in health management. Veterinary services also assist in the control and prevention of livestock and pet diseases in the military establishment, thus protecting both military and civilian populations against tuberculosis, rabies, and other diseases transmissible to humans.

These responsibilities are not confined to the United States. In military bases around the world, veterinarians are working with local public health officials and livestock agencies in raising the standards of animal production and in improving the processing and distribution of food products. Similarly, they are engaged in projects that ultimately protect people from the transmissible diseases prevalent in the area.

Army veterinarians are also on the vanguard of biomedical research. They are currently working on numerous vaccines, antitoxins, and antidotes that will protect both soldiers and civilians.

DOGS AND HORSES

Army veterinarians are also in charge of the health of military working dogs. These dogs are trained by handlers from the military police to hunt down drugs and contraband, as well as to patrol. Canines also participate in search and rescue missions, locating people in buildings that have been destroyed by natural or man-made disasters.

Other Army veterinarians care for the five thousand horses in the cavalry unit at Fort Hood, Texas, and the horses used in the changing of the guard at Arlington National Cemetery.

Army veterinarians also have been called on to help in humanitarian relief efforts, assisting with the evacuation of privately owned pets from hurricane, flood, and earthquake disasters. They were even involved in the evacuation of Clark Air Base in the Philippines following the volcanic eruption of Mount Pinatubo.

91T TRAINING

Another option for a career in military veterinary medicine is the 91T animal care specialist position. The Department of Veterinary Science, part of the U.S. Army Veterinary Medicine School at Fort Sam Houston, trains animal care specialists to fill a wide variety of duties throughout the Department of Defense. Chief among these is tending to the health and maintenance of the military working dogs, which are used for patrolling and sniffing out drugs and explosives. The Army also assigns animal care specialists to work at the military research facilities, overseeing the humane care and treatment of research animals. Animal care specialists also are involved in the fight to control zoonotic diseases and animal-related community health problems. To do this, the 91T personnel provide client education and animal immunization and health care to the privately owned animals of U.S. military personnel throughout the world.

The 91T position offers unique opportunities for those who wish to work with animals other than dogs, cats, and research animals. In recent years, animal care specialists have also tended to marine animals, such as dolphins and porpoises trained by the Navy, as well as horses, mules, farm animals, and birds.

CHAPTER 9

RELATED CAREERS: VETERINARY TECHNICIANS AND OTHER PARAMEDICAL PERSONNEL

As the practice of veterinary medicine enters the twenty-first century, there is a growing need for trained support staff to assist veterinarians in providing the cutting-edge veterinary care that we have begun to expect. The trained veterinary technician (VT) assists veterinarians, biomedical researchers, and other scientists much as nurses and other professionals provide support for doctors.

Veterinary technician training includes education in the care and handling of animals and routine laboratory and clinical procedures. In most private practices, the veterinary technician works as an integral member of the veterinary medical team. This may include obtaining and recording patient case histories; collecting specimens and performing laboratory tests; dressing wounds; taking X rays; preparing patients and instruments for surgery; and assisting with diagnostic, medical, and surgical procedures. Another important role for the veterinary technician is communicating with owners, giving them accurate and complete information regarding the state of their animal, while being sensitive to their concerns.

Veterinary technicians who work for biomedical research facilities may perform a number of the same tasks, as well as supervise the care and handling of animals and assist with the implementation of research projects.

All of the responsibilities of a veterinary technician are performed under the supervision of a veterinarian. The majority of veterinary technicians work for private practices, although others find employment in veterinary-supplies sales, humane societies, and zoos and wildlife facilities.

If veterinary technicians choose to practice at a biological research laboratory, zoo, drug manufacturing company, or meatpacking facility, their responsibilities might include record keeping, animal care, feeding, laboratory procedures, and carcass inspection.

No matter where veterinary technicians choose to work, patience, compassion, and a willingness to be part of a team are important attributes to have. Technicians must also remember that when they graduate, they will be knowledgeable about common domestic animals and familiar with drug names and common laboratory procedures. However, the veterinarians they work with will teach specific procedures and provide information that is appropriate to the specific place of employment.

EDUCATION AND EMPLOYMENT

In 1999 there were more than seventy-five schools accredited by the American Veterinary Medical Association to offer programs in veterinary technology (see Appendix B for a list of these schools). Most of the programs offered are two-year associate degree programs.

In the late 1990s there were more than thirty thousand veterinary technicians employed in the United States, and the number continues to rise with the increase in companion animals. The work site of the veterinary technicians employed is divided in the following way: 59 percent in small-animal practice, 13 percent in research and diagnostic labs, 10 percent in mixed-animal practice, 4 percent in equine practice, 3 percent in education, and others in much smaller numbers.

CURRICULUM AND LICENSING REQUIREMENTS

The core curriculum that accredited schools must follow includes classes in chemistry, applied mathematics, communication skills, humanities or liberal arts, and biological science. To enroll in a veterinary technician program, most schools require a high school diploma or equivalency certificate. Some programs require prerequisite high school or college courses. Other programs consider other factors including aptitude, interest, and ability to benefit from the courses offered.

Most states require veterinary technicians to be registered or certified. Candidates are usually required to take an examination. The process is overseen by the State Board of Veterinary Medical Examiners or other appropriate agency. Many states also require veterinary technicians to pass the Veterinary Technician National Examination. Technicians should follow the specific registration provisions that are set up in their state. The Laboratory Animal Technician Certification Board provides examinations for technicians who are eligible and employed by laboratory facilities.

SALARIES AND CAREER TRACKS

The salaries for veterinary technicians are generally low. Nevertheless, many of the nonmonetary rewards are great, especially for people who enjoy working with animals. In 1999 the average salary for veterinary technicians was $17,000. Those who worked exclusively with small animals earned an average of $22,000; with equines exclusively, an average of $18,000. Earnings in research were a little higher on average at $26,000, while those in industry and sales earned an average of $29,000.

CHAPTER 10

VETERINARY ORGANIZATIONS

THE AMERICAN VETERINARY
MEDICAL ASSOCIATION

The American Veterinary Medical Association (AVMA), a professional organization composed of American and Canadian veterinarians, was founded in 1863. The association, headquartered in Schaumburg, Illinois, has more than sixty-four thousand members working in a wide variety of professional activities.

The objective of the AVMA is to advance the science and art of veterinary medicine, including its relationship to public health, biological science, and agriculture. The AVMA provides a forum for the discussion of issues of importance to the veterinary profession and for the development of official positions. The AVMA is the authorized voice of the profession in presenting its views to government, academia, agriculture, pet owners, the media, and other concerned publics.

The work of the AVMA is directed toward education, licensure, practice, and the many problems and challenges of the profession. In the past, the AVMA has given leadership and guidance in the formulation and enactment of veterinary practice acts, in the formation of state boards of veterinary medical examiners, in the improvement of status and qualifications of those serving in a professional veterinary capacity in the military services, in the founding of veterinary branches of the Public Health Service, and numerous significant contributions to many other advances in the veterinary profession.

AVMA Activities

In addition to the annual meeting of the AVMA, which includes a business meeting and a scientific program, the organization also sponsors other scientific meetings and conferences, publishes two journals, and collaborates in various ways with related professional and scientific organizations in the study of mutual problems. The AVMA also sponsors student chapters in each of the veterinary colleges.

Membership

The membership of the AVMA represents over 80 percent of the active veterinarians in the United States. Each year approximately twenty-one hundred new graduates enter the profession from AVMA-accredited colleges of veterinary medicine.

Membership in the AVMA is categorized as "active," "other members," and "tenure." Active members in the association are those graduates of colleges and schools of veterinary medicine who meet the qualifications specified from time to time in the bylaws of the association.

Other members include honor roll members, affiliate members, and associate members. Tenure members are members who are no longer practicing medicine.

Members of the AVMA follow the guidelines set by the Principles of Veterinary Medical Ethics. These guidelines include issues such as professional behavior; fees for service; emergency service; frauds; genetic defects; determination of therapy, drug, chemical, and alcohol abuse; confidentiality; and others.

U.S. ANIMAL HEALTH ASSOCIATION

Founded in 1897, the USAHA is now a nationwide organization of state and federal livestock officials, ranchers, farmers, and others interested in disease control and eradication. The association studies and disseminates information regarding meat and milk hygiene, including laws, regulations, and policies pertaining to these subjects, and concerning the prevention, control, and eradication of transmissible livestock diseases. Thus it serves as a coordinating agency serving livestock owners, sanitarians, veterinary practitioners, stockyards, auction market and transportation company representatives, producers and processors of meat and milk products, and other related agencies.

Committee Responsibilities

The USAHA conducts much of its business through a committee system. The association has thirty-three active committees, eight of which are species-oriented and twenty-four of which are subject-oriented. The species-oriented committees include: Aquaculture; Captive Wildlife and Alternative Livestock; Infectious Diseases of Cattle, Bison and Llama; Infectious Diseases of Horses, Sheep and Goats; Transmissible Diseases of Poultry and Other Avian Species; Transmissible Diseases of Swine; and Wildlife Diseases.

The subject-oriented committees include: Animal Health Information Systems; Animal Welfare; Biologics and Biotechnology; Bluetongue and Bovine Retrovirus; Brucellosis; Environmental Residues; Epizootic Attack; Feed Safety; Food Safety; Foreign Animal Diseases; Government Relations; Import-Export; Johne's Disease; Livestock Identification; Nominations and Resolutions; Parasitic and Hemoparasitic Diseases and Parasiticides; Pharmaceuticals; Program; Pseudorabies; Public Health and Environmental Quality; Public Relations and Communications Technology; Rabies; Salmonella; Salmonella Enteritidis (SE) in Eggs; and Tuberculosis.

The membership on these committees is integrated to include veterinarians engaged in teaching, research, extension, regulatory work, and practice as well as producers engaged in various livestock operations.

The committees convey their findings and recommendations to the Executive Committee composed of the state livestock officials from each state and representatives of Departments of Agriculture of the United States and Canada. These reports have often been adopted and implemented as the official program for the control and eradication of infectious diseases, such as tick fever, glanders, vesicular exanthema, foot-and-mouth disease, tuberculosis, brucellosis, and pullorum disease in poultry.

OTHER ORGANIZATIONS

Many organizations are geared to individuals either working in or interested in veterinary medicine. Some of those of national and international prominence are listed in Appendix C.

CHAPTER 11

FUTURE TRENDS IN VETERINARY MEDICINE

During the past fifty years, the veterinary profession has expanded its horizons far beyond those envisioned by the most astute pre–World War II "prophets." The ever-broadening scope of veterinary medical services now encompasses such disciplines as space medicine, radiobiology, laboratory animal medicine, bioengineering, toxicology, and many other fields. More and more, veterinarians play a central role in protecting and promoting human health through research and monitoring of animals.

By the year 2000, there were more than fifty-seven thousand veterinarians working in the United States. And the future outlook for veterinarians looks bright, as the field is expected to grow through the first decade or so of the twenty-first century. Even though the number of pets is expected to level off as the population ages, the pets we have will receive better and more sophisticated care as people begin to demand advanced treatments for their companion animals.

Along with the rise in household pets, there has been a tremendous increase in horse ownership. In 1999 there were more than 6,180,000 horses in the United States. The larger numbers call for more equine veterinarians to care for them and to supervise breeding programs. One drawback of equine practice, however, is that the cost of liability insurance for equine practitioners is about ten times that for other self-employed veterinarians.

The next decade also will see changes in the role of the military veterinarian. The military veterinarian has had an impact on both the domestic and foreign front with regard to bioastronautics, radiobiology, food sanitation, research, and many other phases of health-related activities. Today in the U.S. Army Veterinary Corps, veterinarians continue to fill these roles, but they are also involved in new tasks, such as supervising human/animal bond programs at Department of Defense therapy programs. Other responsibilities include ongoing work with ceremonial horses as well as new challenges working with marine mammals.

Finally, industrial development in the production, sales, and research of drugs, chemicals, antibiotics, biologicals, and other therapeutic and diagnostic agents for veterinary use will continue at a very fast pace. Veterinarians trained in virology, bacteriology, biochemistry, parasitology, toxicology, radiology, pathology, and in similar disciplines, as well as in business management and communications, will be in demand by these organizations.

COLLEGES OF VETERINARY MEDICINE

All schools have full accreditation by the American Veterinary Medical Association, unless otherwise noted.

U.S. SCHOOLS

Alabama

Auburn University
  College of Veterinary
    Medicine
  Auburn University, AL 36849
  www.vetmed.auburn.edu

Tuskegee University
  School of Veterinary Medicine
  Tuskegee, AL 36088
  www.tusk.edu

California

University of California
  School of Veterinary Medicine
  Davis, CA 95616-8734
  Limited Accreditation
  www.vetmed.ucdavis.edu

Colorado

Colorado State University
  College of Veterinary
    Medicine and Biomedical
    Sciences
  Fort Collins, CO 80523
  www.cvmbs.colostate.edu

Florida

University of Florida
  College of Veterinary
    Medicine
  Gainesville, FL 32610-0125
  www.vetmed.ufl.edu

Georgia

University of Georgia
  College of Veterinary
    Medicine
  Athens, GA 30602
  www.vet.uga.edu

Illinois

University of Illinois
  College of Veterinary
    Medicine
  2001 S. Lincoln
  Urbana, IL 61801
  www.cvm.uiuc.edu

Indiana

Purdue University
  School of Veterinary Medicine
  1240 Lynn Hall
  West Lafayette, IN 47907-
    1240
  www.vet.purdue.edu

Iowa

Iowa State University
  College of Veterinary
    Medicine
  Ames, IA 50011
  www.vetmed.iastate.edu

Kansas

Kansas State University
  College of Veterinary
    Medicine
  Manhattan, KS 66506
  www.vet.ksu.edu

Louisiana

Louisiana State University
  School of Veterinary Medicine
  Baton Rouge, LA 70803
  www.vetmed.lsu.edu

Massachusetts

Tufts University
  School of Veterinary Medicine
  200 Westboro Rd.
  North Grafton, MA 01536
  www.tufts.edu/vet

Michigan

Michigan State University
  College of Veterinary
    Medicine
  East Lansing, MI 48824-1314
  www.cvm.msu.edu

124   *Opportunities in Veterinary Medicine Careers*

Minnesota

The University of Minnesota
    College of Veterinary
        Medicine
    St. Paul, MN 55108
    www.cvm.umn.edu

Mississippi

Mississippi State University
    College of Veterinary
        Medicine
    Mississippi State, MS 39762
    www.cvm.msstate.edu

Missouri

University of Missouri
    College of Veterinary
        Medicine
    Columbia, MO 65211
    www.cvm.missouri.edu

New York

Cornell University
    College of Veterinary
        Medicine
    Ithaca, NY 14853-6401
    www.vet.cornell.edu

North Carolina

North Carolina State University
    College of Veterinary
        Medicine
    4700 Hillsborough St.
    Raleigh, NC 27606
    www2.ncsu.edu/

Ohio

The Ohio State University
    College of Veterinary
        Medicine
    Columbus, OH 43210
    www.vet.ohio-state.edu

Oklahoma

Oklahoma State University
    College of Veterinary
        Medicine
    Stillwater, OK 74078
    www.cvm.okstate.edu

Oregon

Oregon State University
    College of Veterinary
        Medicine
    Corvallis, OR 97331-4801
    Limited accreditation
    www.vet.orst.edu

Pennsylvania

University of Pennsylvania
  School of Veterinary Medicine
  3800 Spruce St.
  Philadelphia, PA 19104-6044
  www.vet.upenn.edu

Tennessee

University of Tennessee
  College of Veterinary
    Medicine
  Knoxville, TN 37901
  www.vet.utk.edu

Texas

Texas A&M University
  College of Veterinary
    Medicine
  College Station, TX 77843-
    4461
  www.cvm.tamu.edu

Virginia

Virginia Tech and University of
    Maryland
  Virginia-Maryland Regional
    College of Veterinary
    Medicine
  Blacksburg, VA 24061-0442
  www.vetmed.vt.edu

Washington

Washington State University
  College of Veterinary
    Medicine
  Pullman, WA 99164-7010
  www.vetmed.wsu.edu

Wisconsin

The University of Wisconsin-
    Madison
  School of Veterinary Medicine
  Madison, WI 53706
  www.vetmed.wisc.edu

CANADIAN SCHOOLS

Guelph, Ontario

Ontario Veterinary College
  University of Guelph
  Guelph, Ontario
  Canada N1G 2W1

Charlottetown, Prince Edward Island

University of Prince Edward
    Island
  Atlantic Veterinary College
  Charlottetown, Prince Edward
    Island
  Canada C1A 4P3

Montreal, Quebec

University of Montreal
  Faculty of Veterinary
    Medicine
  Saint Hyacinthe, Quebec
  Canada J2S 7C6
  Limited Accreditation

Saskatoon, Saskatchewan

University of Saskatchewan
  Western College of Veterinary
    Medicine
  52 Campus Dr.
  Saskatoon, Saskatchewan
  Canada S7N 5B4

PROGRAMS IN VETERINARY TECHNOLOGY

All courses, unless otherwise noted, are two-year Associate in Science programs with full accreditation by the American Veterinary Medical Association Committee on Veterinary Technician Education and Activities (CVTEA).

"Full accreditation" means that those programs meet or exceed the minimal requirements. "Provisional accreditation" is given to programs that meet or exceed most, but not all, minimal requirements and that have not produced graduates. "Probational accreditation" signifies that a program meets or exceeds most, but not all, minimal requirements.

The following do not have AVMA-accredited veterinary technology programs: Alaska, Arizona, Arkansas, Delaware, District of Columbia, Hawaii, Maine, Montana, Nevada, New Mexico, and Rhode Island.

Alabama

Snead State Community College
  Veterinary Technology
    Program
  Boaz, AL 35957
  www.boaz.net/sneadstate

California

California State Polytechnic
    University
  College of Agriculture
  Animal Health Technology
    Program
  3801 W. Temple Ave.
  Pomona, CA 91768
  www.csupomona.edu/~agri/
    catalog/
    veterinary_sciences.htm
  4 years, Bachelor of Science;
    Probational accreditation

Cosumnes River College
  Veterinary Technology
    Program
  8401 Center Pkwy.
  Sacramento, CA 95823
  www.crc.losrios.cc.ca.us/
    welcome.html

Foothill College
  Veterinary Technology
    Program
  12345 El Monte Rd.
  Los Altos Hills, CA 94022
  www.foothill.fhda.edu/bio/
    programs/vettech/
    index.shtml

Hartnell College
  Animal Health Technology
    Program
  156 Homestead Ave.
  Salinas, CA 93901
  www.hartnell.cc.ca.us/
    degrees/animal_health_
    technology.html

Los Angeles Pierce College
  Veterinary Technology
    Program
  6201 Winnetka Ave.
  Woodland Hills, CA 91371
  www.macrohead.com/rvt/

Mt. San Antonio College
  Animal Health Technology
    Program
  1100 N. Grand Ave.
  Walnut, CA 91789
  www.mtsac.edu/

Yuba College
Veterinary Technology
Program
2088 N. Beale Rd.
Marysville, CA 95901
www.ms.yuba.cc.ca.us/
~brussell

Colorado

Bel-Rea Institute of Animal
Technology
1681 S. Dayton St.
Denver, CO 80231
www.bel-rea.com

Colorado Mountain College
Veterinary Technology
Program
Spring Valley Campus
3000 County Rd. 114
Glenwood Springs, CO 81601
www.coloradomtn.edu/
programs/aas_vet_tech.
html

Front Range Commmunity
College
Veterinary Research
Technology Program
4616 S. Shields
Ft. Collins, CO 80526
www.frcc.cc.co.us/about/
pubs/cat/programs/
veterinary_research.html
Probational accreditation

Connecticut

NW Connecticut Community
Technical College
Veterinary Technology
Program
Park Place East
Winstead, CT 06098
Probational accreditation

Quinnipiac College
Veterinary Technology
Program
Mt. Carmel Ave.
Hamden, CT 06518
www.quinnipiac.edu/
academics/degree_
programs.asp

Florida

Brevard Community College
Veterinary Technology
Program
1519 Clearlake Rd.
Cocoa, FL 32922
Probational accreditation

St. Petersburg Junior College
Veterinary Technology
Program
Box 13489
St. Petersburg, FL 33733
www.hec.spjc.cc.fl.us/chip/
vt1.html

Georgia

Gwinnett Technical Institute
Veterinary Technology
Program
5150 Sugarloaf Pkwy.
Lawrenceville, GA 30043
Probational accreditation

Fort Valley State College
Veterinary Technology
Program
Fort Valley, GA 31030
www.agschool.fvsc.
peachnet.edu/html/
instruction/veterinary-
technology/overview.htm
Probational accreditation

Idaho

College of Southern Idaho
Veterinary Technology
Program
315 Falls Ave.
Twin Falls, ID 83303-1238
Probational accreditation

Illinois

Parkland College
Veterinary Technology
Program
2400 W. Bradley Ave.
Champaign, IL 61821
www.parkland.cc.il.us/hp/
vtt.htm

Indiana

Purdue University
School of Veterinary Medicine
Veterinary Technology
Program
West Lafayette, IN 47907
www.ecn.www.ecn.
purdue.edu/ecn/course.
catalogs/vetmed/vm.tech.
pos.html
4 years, Bachelor of Science

Iowa

Kirkwood Community College
Veterinary Technician
Program
6301 Kirkwood Blvd., SW
Cedar Rapids, IA 52406
www.kirkwood.cc.ia.us/
agrisciences/vettech.html

Kansas

Colby Community College
Veterinary Technology
Program
1255 S. Range
Colby, KS 67701
www.colby.cc.ks.us: 8000/
www/vet/vettech.html

Kentucky

Morehead State University
Veterinary Technology
Program
25 MSU Farm Dr.
Morehead, KY 40351
www.morehead-st.edu/
prospects/study/
undergraduate/vettechs/
index.html

Murray State University
Animal Health Technology
Program
Department of Agriculture
Murray, KY 42071
www.murraystate.edu/
4 years, Bachelor of Science

Louisiana

Northwestern State University of
Louisiana
Veterinary Technology
Program
Department of Life Sciences
Natchitoches, LA 71497
www.vic.nsula.edu/

Maryland

Essex Community College
Veterinary Technology
Program
7201 Rossville Blvd.
Baltimore, MD 21237
www.ccbc.ccmd.us/

Massachusetts

Becker College
Veterinary Technology
Program
3 Paxton St.
Leicester, MA 01524
www.beckercollege.com

Holyoke Community College
Veterinary Technician
Program
303 Homestead Ave.
Holyoke, MA 01040-1099

Mt. Ida College
Veterinary Technician
Program
777 Dedham St.
Newton Center, MA 02159
www.mountida.edu/
admissions/sch_asci.html
3 years, Associate in Science;
4 years, Bachelor of
Science

Michigan

Macomb Community College
Veterinary Technician
Program
Center Campus
44575 Garfield Rd.
Clinton Township, MI 48044
www.macomb.cc.mi.us/
default.htm

Michigan State University
  College of Veterinary
    Medicine
  Veterinary Technology
    Program
  East Lansing, MI 48823
  www.cvm.msu.edu/education/
    vet_tech.htm
  2 years, Associate in Applied
    Science; 4 years, Bachelor
    of Science

Wayne County Community
    College
  Veterinary Technology
    Program
  c/o Wayne State University
  Division of Laboratory
    Animal Resources
  540 E. Canfield
  Detroit, MI 48201
  www.sun2.science.
    wayne.edu/

Minnesota

Medical Institute of Minnesota
  Veterinary Technician
    Program
  5503 Green Valley Dr.
  Bloomington, MN 55437
  www.mim.tec.mn.us/
  19 months, Associate in
    Applied Science

Ridgewater College
  Veterinary Technology
    Department
  2101 15th Ave., NW
  Willmar, MN 56201
  www.ridgewater.mnscu.
    edu/

Mississippi

Hinds Community College
  Veterinary Technology
    Program
  P.O. Box 10461
  Raymond, MS 39154
  www.cvm.msstate.edu/
    academics/

Missouri

Jefferson College
  Veterinary Technology
    Program
  1000 Viking Dr.
  Hillsboro, MO 63050
  www.jeffco.edu/veterina.htm

Maple Woods Community
    College
  Veterinary Technology
    Program
  2601 NE Barry Rd.
  Kansas City, MO 64156
  www.kcmetro.cc.mo.us/
    specialprog/vettech.html

Nebraska

Nebraska College of Technical
Agriculture
Veterinary Technology
Program
Curtis, NE 69025
www.ianr.unl.edu/ncta/vt/
vtech.html
2 years, Associate in
Technical Agriculture in
Veterinary Technology

Northeast Community College
Veterinary Technology
Program
801 E. Benjamin Ave.
Norfolk, NE 68702-0469
Probational accreditation

Omaha College of Health
Careers
Veterinary Technician
Program
225 N. 80th St.
Omaha, NE 68114
18 months, Associate in
Applied Science

New Hampshire

New Hampshire Community
Technical College
Veterinary Technology
Program
227 Portsmouth Ave.
Stratham, NH 03885-2297
www.stratham.tec.nh.us/
Probational accreditation

New Jersey

Camden County College
Animal Science Technology
Program
P.O. Box 200
Blackwood, NJ 08012
www.camdencc.edu/
departments/animal%20
science/home3.htm

New York

La Guardia Community College
The City University of New
York
Veterinary Technology
Program
31-10 Thomson Ave.
Long Island City, NY 11101
www.lagcc.cuny.edu/nas/
nas2o.htm

Medaille College
Veterinary Technology
Program
18 Agassiz Cr.
Buffalo, NY 14214
www.medaille.edu/vt.html

Mercy College
Veterinary Technology
Program
555 Broadway
Dobbs Ferry, NY 10522
www.mercynet.edu/
4 years, Bachelor of Science

State University of New York
Agricultural & Technical
College
Health Sciences & Medical
Technologies
Veterinary Science
Technology Program
Canton, NY 13617

State University of New York
College of Technology
Veterinary Science
Technology Program
Delhi, NY 13753
www.delhi.edu/page/vettech/
index.htm

Suffolk Community College
Veterinary Science
Technology Program
Western Campus
Crooked Hill Rd.
Brentwood, NY 11717
www.sunysuffolk.edu/
programs/390-1.shtml

North Carolina

Central Carolina Community
College
Veterinary Medical
Technology Program
1105 Kelly Dr.
Sanford, NC 27330
www.ccarolina.cc.nc.us/

Gaston College
Veterinary Medical
Technology Program
201 Hwy. 321 South
Dallas, NC 28034-1499
www.gaston.cc.nc.us/

North Dakota

North Dakota State University
Veterinary Technology
Program
Department of Veterinary
Science
Fargo, ND 58105
www.cc.ndsu.nodak.edu/
instruct/devold/vetmicro/
vettech.htm
4 years, Bachelor of Science

Ohio

Columbus State Community
College
Veterinary Technology
Program
550 E. Spring St.
Columbus, OH 43216
www.colstate.cc.oh.us/docs/
vetcurr.htm

Cuyahoga Community College
  Veterinary Technology
    Program
  11000 Pleasant Valley Rd.
  Parma, OH 44130
  www.tri-c.cc.oh.us/health/
    index.htm
  Provisional accreditation

Stautzenberger College
  Veterinary Technology
    Program
  5355 S. Wyck
  Toledo, OH 43614
  Probational accreditation

UC Raymond Walters College
  Veterinary Technology
    Program
  P.O. Box 670571
  Cincinnati, OH 45267-0571
  www.rwc.uc.edu/academic/
    vettech/vettinfo.htm

Oklahoma

Murray State College
  Veterinary Technology
    Program
  Tishomingo, OK 73460
  www.msc.cc.ok.us/acad/
    vettech/main.htm

Oklahoma State University
  Veterinary Technology
    Program
  900 N. Portland Ave.
  Oklahoma City, OK 73107
  Provisional accreditation

Tulsa Community College
  Veterinary Technology
    Program
  7505 W. 41st St.
  Tulsa, OK 74107
  2 years, Associate in Applied
    Science; Provisional
    accreditation

Oregon

Portland Community College
  Veterinary Technology
    Program
  P.O. Box 19000
  Portland, OR 97219
  www.pcc.edu/academ/vettech/

Pennsylvania

Harcum College
  Veterinary Technology
    Program
  750 Montgomery Ave.
  Bryn Mawr, PA 19010-3476
  www.harcum.edu/programs
  6 semesters, Associate in
    Science

Johnson Technical Institute
    Veterinary Science
        Technology Program
    3427 N. Main Ave.
    Scranton, PA 18505
    www.jti.org/iii-m.htm
    Probational accreditation

Lehigh Carbon & Northampton
        Community Colleges
    Veterinary Technology
        Program
    3835 Green Pond Rd.
    Bethlehem, PA 18020
    Probational accreditation

Manor College
    Veterinary Technology
        Program
    Fox Chase Rd. & Forest Ave.
    Jenkintown, PA 19046
    www.manor.edu/.\vt-program/
        index.htm

Wilson College
    Veterinary Medical
        Technology Program
    Chambersburg, PA 17201
    www.wilson.edu/
    4 years, Bachelor of Science,
        College for Women; 2
        years, Associate in Science,
        Continuing Studies
        Division

Puerto Rico

University of Puerto Rico
    Veterinary Technology
        Program
    Medical Sciences Campus
    P.O. Box 365067
    San Juan, PR 00936-5067
    www.upr.clu.edu/englishv2/
    4 years, Bachelor of Science

South Carolina

Newberry College
    Veterinary Technology
        Program
    2100 College St.
    Newberry, SC 29108
    4 years, Bachelor of Science;
        Probational accreditation

Tri-County Technical College
    Veterinary Technology
        Program
    P.O. Box 587
    Pendleton, SC 29670
    2 years, Associate in Health
        Science

South Dakota

National American University
Allied Health Division
Veterinary Technology
Program
321 Kansas City St.
Rapid City, SD 57709
www.nationalcollege.edu/
vet.html
8 quarters, Associate in
Applied Science

Tennessee

Columbia State Community
College
Veterinary Technology
Program
Columbia, TN 38401
www.coscc.cc.tn.us/academic/
acadoffn.htm

Lincoln Memorial University
Veterinary Technology
Program
Harrogate, TN 37752
www.lmunet.edu/

Texas

Cedar Valley College
Veterinary Technology
Program
3030 N. Dallas Ave.
Lancaster, TX 75134
www.texasusa.com/
commshow/lancastr/
cvcvet.html

Midland College
Veterinary Technology
Program
3600 N. Garfield
Midland, TX 79705
www.midland.cc.tx.us/
tech.html
Probational accreditation

Palo Alto College
Veterinary Technology
Program
1400 W. Villaret Blvd.
San Antonio, TX 78224-2499
www.accd.edu/pac/agri/
vett.htm
Probational accreditation

Sul Ross State University
School of Agriculture &
Natural Resource Sciences
Veterinary Technology
Program
Alpine, TX 79830
www.sulross.edu/

Tomball College
Veterinary Technology
Program
30555 Tomball Pkwy.
Tomball, TX 77375-4036
www.tc.nhmccd.edu/

Utah

Brigham Young University
  Veterinary Technology
    Program
  Provo, UT 84602
  www.bioag.byu.edu/anisci/
  4 years, Bachelor in Animal
    Science

Vermont

Vermont Technical College
  Veterinary Technology
    Program
  Randolph Center, VT 05061
  www.vtc.vsc.edu/

Virginia

Blue Ridge Community College
  Veterinary Technology
    Program
  Box 80
  Weyers Cave, VA 24486

Northern Virginia Community
    College
  Veterinary Technology
    Program
  Loudoun Campus
  1000 Harry Flood Byrd Hwy.
  Sterling, VA 20164-8699

Washington

Pierce College at Ft. Steilacoom
  Veterinary Technology
    Program
  9401 Farwest Dr., SW
  Lakewood, WA 98498
  www.pierce.ctc.edu/
  2 years, Associate in Animal
    Technology

Yakima Valley Community
    College
  Veterinary Technology
    Program
  P.O. Box 1647
  Yakima, WA 98907-1647
  www.yvcc.cc.wa.us/pace/ag/
    vetech.htm
  Probational accreditation

West Virginia

Fairmont State College
  Veterinary Technology
    Program
  Fairmont, WV 26554
  www.fscwv.edu/hc/vettech/
    vtech_hp.html

Wisconsin

Madison Area Technical College
  Veterinary Technician
    Program
  3550 Anderson
  Madison, WI 53704
  www.madison.tec.wi.us/
    catalog/pages/
    matchome.html

Wyoming

Eastern Wyoming College
  Veterinary Technology
    Program
  3200 W. "C" St.
  Torrington, WY 82240
  www.ewcweb.ewc.
    whecn. edu/

Canadian Veterinary Technology Programs (Non-AVMA Accredited)

For more information regarding Canadian veterinary technology programs, contact:

Canadian Association of Animal
    Health Technologists &
    Technicians
  Box 91
  Grandora, Saskatchewan
  Canada S0K 1V0

VETERINARY SPECIALTY ORGANIZATIONS

American Board of Veterinary
   Practitioners
530 Church St., Suite 700
Nashville, TN 37219

American Board of Veterinary
   Toxicology
University of Pennsylvania
New Bolton Center
382 W. Street Rd.
Kennett Square, PA 19348

American College of Laboratory
   Animal Medicine
96 Chester St.
Chester, NH 03036

American College of Poultry
   Veterinarians
P.O. Box 1227
Fayetteville, AR 72702

American College of
   Theriogenologists
530 Church St., Suite 700
Nashville, TN 37219

American College of Veterinary
   Anesthesiologists
Department of Surgical &
   Radiological Sciences
School of Veterinary Medicine
University of California
Davis, CA 95616-8745

American College of Veterinary
   Behaviorists
Department of Small Animal
   Medicine & Surgery
Texas A&M University
College Station, TX 77843-
   4474

American College of Veterinary
Clinical Pharmacology
Department of Anatomy,
Pathology & Pharmacology
College of Veterinary
Medicine
Oklahoma State University
Stillwater, OK 74078

American College of Veterinary
Dermatology
2122 Worthingwoods Blvd.
Powell, OH 43065

American College of Veterinary
Emergency and Critical
Care
Department of Clinical
Sciences
School of Veterinary Medicine
Tufts University
200 Westboro Rd.
North Grafton, MA 01536

American College of Veterinary
Internal Medicine
1997 Wadsworth Blvd.,
Suite A
Lakewood, CO 80215-3327

American College of Veterinary
Microbiologists
College of Veterinary
Medicine
P.O. Box 1071
University of Tennessee
Knoxville, TN 37901

American College of Veterinary
Nutrition
Large Animal Clinical
Sciences
Virginia-Maryland Regional
College of Veterinary
Medicine
Blacksburg, VA 24061-0442

American College of Veterinary
Ophthalmologists
Veterinary Clinical Sciences
Louisiana State University
Baton Rouge, LA 70803

American College of Veterinary
Pathologists
ACVP Executive Offices
875 Kings Hwy., Suite 200
Woodbury, NJ 08096-3172

American College of Veterinary
Preventive Medicine
3126 Morning Creek
San Antonio, TX 78247

American College of Veterinary
Radiology
P.O. Box 87
Glencoe, IL 60022

American College of Veterinary
Surgeons
4401 East West Hwy, Suite
205
Bethesda, MD 20814-4523

American College of Zoological
Medicine
White Oak Conservation
Center
White Oak Plantation
726 Owens Rd.
Yulee, FL 32097

American Veterinary Dental
College
Department of Surgical &
Radiological Sciences
School of Veterinary Medicine
University of California
Davis, CA 95616-8745

VETERINARY PUBLICATIONS

American Journal of Veterinary Research
1931 Meacham Rd., #100
Schaumburg, IL 60173
American Veterinary Medical Association

California Veterinarian
5231 Madison Ave.
Sacramento, CA 95841
California Veterinary Medical Association

DVM, The Newsmagazine of Veterinary Medicine
7500 Old Oak Blvd.
Cleveland, OH 44130
Advanstar Communications, Inc.

Equine Veterinary Data
20225 Grand Ave.
Wildomar, CA 92595
Veterinary Data

Equine Veterinary Journal
425 Phillips Blvd., #100
Trenton, NJ 08618
Veterinary Learning Systems Co., Inc.

Journal of the American Animal Hospital Association
12575 W. Bayaud Ave.
Lakewood, CO 80228
American Animal Hospital Association

Journal of American Veterinary Medical Association
1931 Meacham Rd., #100
Schaumburg, IL 60173
American Veterinary Medical Association

The Journal of Equine Veterinary Science
20225 Grand Ave.
Wildomar, CA 92595
Veterinary Data

Lab Animal
345 Park Ave. South
New York, NY 10010

Large Animal Veterinary Report
20225 Grand Ave.
Wildomar, CA 92595
Veterinary Data

Pulse
8338 S. Rosemead Blvd.
Pico Rivera, CA 90660
Southern California
Veterinary Medical
Association

Trends
12575 W. Bayaud Ave.
Lakewood, CO 80228
American Animal Hospital
Association

Veterinary Economics
15333 W. 95th St.
Lenexa, KS 66215
Veterinary Medicine
Publishing Company

Veterinary Forum
425 Phillips Blvd., #100
Trenton, NJ 08618

Veterinary Medicine
5333 W. 95th St.
Lenexa, KS 66215
Veterinary Medicine
Publishing COmpany

Veterinary Practice News
P.O. Box 6050
Mission Viejo, CA 92690
Fancy Publications, Inc.

Veterinary Technician
425 Phillips Blvd., #100
Trenton, NJ 08618
Veterinary Learning Systems

Veterinary Therapeutics
425 Phillips Blvd., #100
Trenton, NJ 08618
Veterinary Learning Systems

GLOSSARY

Agronomy—the study and practice of field crop production and soil management

Anatomy—science and study of the structure of an organism and its parts

Anesthesiology—science and study of the use of anesthesia and anesthetic drugs; medical specialty in the use of drugs and other means to avert or reduce pain in patients especially during surgery

Animal Pathology—the study of animals' diseases

Anthrax—bacterial disease of cattle and other farm animals that can be transmitted to humans from infected animals and animal products

Artificial Insemination—the artificial or mechanical placement of semen into the reproductive tract of a female animal

Avian—pertaining to birds, including poultry

Bacteriology—science and study of bacteria, their development and their effect on human tissue

Bioengineering—branch of biology dealing with processing or artificial production of plant and animal materials, especially in the fermentation of organic products

Brucellosis—disease caused by infection with a bacterium, obtained by association with infected livestock or their products and causing chills, weakness, headache, and recurring fever

Cesarean Section—surgical incision through the abdomen and uterus for removal of a fetus, performed when conditions for normal vaginal delivery are deemed hazardous for mother or baby

Cardiology—medical specialty that involves the study of the heart and diagnosis and treatment of its diseases

Corticosteroids—a group of hormones produced in the adrenal cortex that are important for the metabolism of carbohydrates and proteins, for water and salt balance, and for the function of the cardiovascular system

Encephalitis—inflammation of the brain, usually due to viral infection but sometimes occurring as a complication of another infection or resulting from poison

Epidemiology—the study of the causes, occurrences, and control of disease

Equine—pertaining to horses

Gynecology—medical specialty concerned with the health care of female animals, including function and diseases of the reproductive organs; combines both medical and surgical concerns

Histology—science and study of tissue

Hog Cholera—acute infection with bacterium characterized by severe diarrhea and vomiting, often leading to dehydration, electrolyte imbalances, and, if untreated, death

Immunology—study of the body's response to foreign invasion

Internal Medicine—branch of medicine concerned with the function of internal organs and the diagnosis and treatment of disorders affecting these organs

Large-Animal Veterinarian—one who practices on farm animals: for example, cattle, hogs, sheep, or horses

Leptospirosis—infection caused by a spirochete transmitted to humans from infected animals often from their urine

Microbiology—branch of biology concerned with the study of microorganisms, including bacteria, viruses, rickettsiae, fungi, and protozoa

Mycology—the study of fungi and fungus-caused diseases

Neurology—branch of medicine concerned with the structure, function, and diseases of the nervous system

Obstetrics—branch of medicine concerned with the care of female animals during pregnancy, childbirth, and the immediate postpartum period

Ophthalmology—study of the eye: its development, structure, functions, defects, diseases, and treatment

Orthopedics—branch of medicine concerned with the musculoskeletal system including bones, joints, muscles, ligaments, and tendons and the treatment of disorders affecting it

Parasite—organism that lives in or on another organism, obtaining nourishment from it

Pathology—study of disease, especially the observable effects of disease on body tissue

Pharmaceutical—drug used in medical treatment

Physiology—branch of science dealing with the normal chemical functioning of living organisms

Radiology—the branch of medicine concerned with X rays, radioactive substances, and other imaging techniques, and their use in diagnosis and treatment

Scabies—contagious disease caused by the itch mite and characterized by itching and skin irritation often leading to secondary infection

Serology—branch of science concerned with the study of blood serum, especially the search for evidence of infection and the evaluation of immune reactions

Small-Animal Veterinarian—one who practices on house pets: for example, cats, dogs, or birds

Toxicology—study of poisons and their effects on living organisms

Tuberculosis—chronic infection with bacterium transmitted by inhalation or ingestion of droplets; it usually affects the lungs but may also affect other organs

Virology—study of viruses, their growth, development, and relationship to diseases

Zoonosis—disease of animals that can be transmitted to humans

SELECTED BIBLIOGRAPHY

Careers in focus. *Animal Care.* Chicago: Ferguson Publishing, 1998.

Crawford, Jane Diehl. *The Preveterinary Planning Guide.* Potomac, MD: Betz Pub. Company, 1995.

Drum, Jane C. *Women in Veterinary Medicine: Profiles of Success.* Ames: Iowa State University Press, 1991.

Duncan, Jane Caryl. *Careers in Veterinary Medicine.* New York: Rosen Pub. Group, 1994.

Gage, Loretta. *If Wishes Were Horses: The Education of a Veterinarian.* New York: St. Martin's Press, 1994.

Gutkind, Lee. *An Unspoken Art: Profiles of Veterinary Life.* New York: Henry Holt and Co., 1997.

Herriot, James. *Every Living Thing.* New York: St. Martin's Press, 1994.

Karesh, William B. *Appointment at the Ends of the World: Memoirs of a Wildlife Veterinarian.* New York: Warner Books, 1999.

McBride, Douglas F. *Learning Veterinary Terminology.* St. Louis, MO: Mosby Publishing Company, 1996.

McCarthy, John B., ed. *Planning Your Veterinary Career.* Denver, CO: American Animal Hospital Association, 1992.

McCormack, John E. *A Friend of the Flock: Tales of a Country Veterinarian.* New York: Crown Publishers, 1997.

————. *The Hero of the Herd: More Tales from a Country Veterinarian.* New York: Crown Publishers, 1999.

Smith, M. McCoy. *Never Alone: The Life and Times of a Country Veterinarian.* Nashville, TN: Eggman Publishers, 1995.

Taylor, David. *Vet on the Wild Side.* New York: St. Martin's Press, 1990.

————. *The Patient Elephant: More Exotic Cases from the World's Top Wildlife Vet.* Jersey City, NJ: Robson, London, 1993.

Tufts University. *Animal E.R.: Extraordinary Stories of Hope and Healing from One of the World's Leading Veterinary Hospitals.* New York: Dutton Books, 1999.

Veterinary Medical School Admission Requirements in the United States and Canada. New Orleans, LA: Purdue University Press, 1999.

Ward, F. M. *Reflections of a Veterinarian: Don't Follow Me, I Stepped in Something.* Waco, TX: Texian Press, 1995.